EATERTAINMENT

RECIPES AND IDEAS FOR
EFFORTLESS ENTERTAINING

FROM EASY TO EXTRAVAGANT WITH
SEBASTIEN AND SHEILA CENTNER

appetite
by RANDOM HOUSE

Appetite by Random House® and colophon are registered trademarks of Penguin Random House LLC.

Library and Archives of Canada Cataloguing in Publication is available upon request.

ISBN: 9780525611226

eBook ISBN: 9780525611233

Book design by Jennifer Griffiths

Photography by Bruce Gibson

Printed in China

Published in Canada by Appetite by Random House®, a division of Penguin Random House LLC.

www.penguinrandomhouse.ca

10 9 8 7 6 5 4 3 2 1

appetite
by RANDOM HOUSE

This book is dedicated to our family and friends, who are always willing to fill our table. It's also dedicated to everyone reading this book. May your lives be filled with memories made while enjoying great food and drink with those for whom you care most. Life is meant to be lived, with friends who are like family and family who are also friends, and there is no better way to enjoy life than while entertaining.

Seb + Sheila

CONTENTS

INTRODUCTION

There's a story that we love to tell new friends about how we met, almost 27 years ago. This introduction couldn't possibly accommodate that entire story, especially the way Sebastien tells it, but it sets the backdrop for how we have built our lives and our business and for the passion we try to put into everything we do, like this book, so we'll condense it to a few simple sentences.

It involved a bunch of friends, a club in Toronto, about 60 shooters (not just for us two, of course), and then a lunch and dinner the next day. We've been together ever since. A week after we met, we moved in together, about a month after that we were engaged, and less than one year later, two very young 23- and 24-year-olds tied the knot in the backyard of Sebastien's parents' home. Our friends and family thought we were making a mistake, but we both knew there was something special between us.

Seb is the romantic-pragmatic character in this story, always happy to share how he knew on that first night that we would be together forever. The logic he shared with those who questioned this monumental decision was: you don't marry someone because you think they'll make a good wife or a good mom—you marry someone you can't live without, because that is what will keep the passion alive and get you through the tough times every couple eventually faces.

Sheila is the fun-loving yet matter-of-fact character in this story, always ready to crank up the music, pour everyone a glass of rosé, and set things in motion for a memorable night, even if it happens to be a school night. She has a few favorite sayings that sum up who she is: "If not now, then when?" refers to her ability to look on the bright side of life, regardless of the situation. She is committed to helping those around her achieve happiness and success, and won't let anything stand in her way. When anyone does try to get in her way or present an unsolveable challenge, her response is always, "That sounds like a 'you' problem."

While completely different in so many ways, we are always 100% aligned when it comes to our family, our boys, and our support for one another. This has been our formula for a successful marriage and the foundation on which we have built our businesses over the past two decades.

The best way to understand our approach to life is to watch us host a dinner party. It's a bit like a dance, with each of us always knowing where the other one is (Seb is refilling wine glasses and Sheila is putting the main course in the oven). We come together (as we greet our guests with trays of welcome cocktails and take their coats) and move apart (as Sheila heads to the wine cellar to grab the next bottle of wine and Seb clears the plates from the first course), but we always end up side by side by the end of the evening. We absolutely love to enter-tain, and bringing people together over a great meal gives us tremendous joy. Neither of us is quite sure how we ended up with a similar passion for entertaining, but we're sure that we feed off each other, and that makes hosting a lot easier.

When people join us at home, they often comment on how they could never host like we do—but they couldn't be more wrong! What we do is neither rocket

science nor unachievable. It is simply a little measure of planning, a sprinkling of teamwork, and a good dose of joie de vivre. That's the recipe for great entertaining—along with perhaps a glass or two of rosé!

But the truth is that hosting wasn't always easy for us and we weren't always that good at it. Like anything worthwhile in life, it took a lot of hard work. We failed lots of times. We had many nights where dinners were so badly burned that we had to order in. We ran out of alcohol one New Year's Eve while at a remote cottage. And there were many times we had to do the dishes with Mr. Clean (Seb's mother may not have had him do the dishes often enough when he was growing up). But we learned from each failure, and from each subsequent gathering we built our repertoire of go-to tips, tricks, and recipes that would eventually become the foundation of our entertaining arsenal.

Of course, even now, it's not all rainbows and unicorns—for example, when Sheila sticks to her habit of wanting to clean up every last dish (and then Swiffer) after the guests have left, no matter the time, or when Seb says he wants to help her with the cleanup but grumbles all the way through. . . But beneath the sparkle of the photo shoots and the frantic lifestyle that goes along with running multiple businesses, we're still those two kids who met over a tray of shooters many years ago. We've learned a lot and we've never stopped having fun. This book is about sharing all those learnings with you so that you can entertain without suffering through the frustration that often comes along with hosting.

Sebastien's mother, Maryvone, first inspired his love of hosting. Mavone, as she was known to her grandchildren, was the consummate French hostess, always ready to entertain a group no matter how large or small and no matter how last-minute. Her love of cooking and passion for filling her home with old and new friends made for a rotating door of dinner parties that Sebastien and his brother, Olivier, were fortunate enough to enjoy when they were growing up. There was the time Mavone hosted the going-away party for a local jazz musician who ended up never leaving (thus requiring a "he's not leaving" party the following week during which Mavone ended up in the pool—fully dressed). And of course, there were the countless dinners in the south of France where her signature Dame Blanche dessert became a staple not only because of how delicious it was, but also because she was able to make it even after several glasses of wine. The love of life that Mavone instilled in both of us is something we still celebrate today with the annual Eve Before The Eve holiday dinner, which was inspired by a tradition she started over four decades ago. For us, this element of tradition is how our success in sharing our love of entertaining will be measured. We imagine that, years from now, our boys, Colsen and Logan, will each have their own families and be hosting their own dinner parties. When those days come, we hope they raise their glasses to all the dinner parties and brunches they grew up with and make just as many memories of their own with their families and friends. Hopefully we even get invited to a few of them!

But hosting is not just something we do for fun. We've been fortunate enough to be able to pour all our passion for entertaining into our many businesses, and perhaps that's how this book has ended up in your hands. Maybe you've attended one of the hundreds of Eatertainment events we host each year, or listened to one of our Seb + Sheila Dinner Series playlists, or happened to catch one of our TV segments or videos on social media. In any case, we hope we can show you, through our businesses and through this book, the kind of professional and personal satisfaction we've found through entertaining, and we hope that you're inspired to find that same passion in yourself.

Entertaining should be fun, so make sure to take a step back and enjoy every moment, because the better time you're having, the more your guests will enjoy themselves! And don't forget that your guests are in your home because of YOU, so go with the flow. If you happen to burn the main course, well, there's always takeout.

We hope this book inspires you to call up some friends and invite them for a casual barbecue, formal dinner, or even just cocktails and pizza, because to us, the most important ingredients of any get-together are friends and family!

Seb + Sheila
@sebcentner @sheilacentner @eatertainment @sebandsheila

ENTERTAINING ESSENTIALS

HOW TO USE THIS BOOK

While we wrote this book in ascending order of difficulty, beginning with the easier hosting events and working toward more complex ones, feel free to jump around, as there is no rule that says you have to work through it chapter by chapter.

We've also written recipe yields in this book that reflect the way we like to entertain. For canapés, which are always bite-sized, we plan for six to eight canapés total—even if you are only entertaining for six people, those last two canapés always get snatched up. For family-style dishes, where you'll have a range of appetites, we've created recipes that feed six to eight people. For individually plated dishes, you'll see more specific yields. If you find yourself entertaining more than six or eight people at a time, you can double the recipes. If you're more likely to host a smaller group of four, you'll have leftovers!

We hope this book is one you return to time and time again, either in the spirit of recreating the entire chapters or just to grab the recipe for that delicious lemon tiramisu you get a craving for one night.

A few notes on some of our staple ingredients:

- Eggs are large.
- Unless otherwise noted, butter is unsalted and at room temperature.
- Milk is whole milk.
- Olive oil is extra virgin.
- Vanilla extract is pure.
- Herbs are fresh, unless otherwise noted.
- Black and white pepper are ground, unless otherwise noted.
- Citrus juice is fresh, unless otherwise noted.
- For drinks, lemons and limes are cut in wedges and oranges in slices, unless otherwise noted.
- Ice means ice cubes, unless otherwise noted.

When it comes to seafood, which you'll often find on our menus, we have a few must-know tips and tricks:

- There are many different types of oysters, so if you aren't sure which ones to buy, look for oysters that were harvested as close as possible to you. If you live in the middle of the country, ask your fishmonger, local market, or grocery store when they get their seafood deliveries to find the best time to pick up your order.

- Bigger is not better when it comes to seafood! Smaller lobsters and oysters tend to be tastier than larger ones.

- To keep the ice in your seafood tower trays from melting, put the trays in the freezer for at least 1 hour before you start assembling the towers.

- Shucking oysters takes practice and the right equipment. If you've not done much shucking, invest in a steel mesh shucking glove.

SETTING THE TABLE

Preparation is key when it comes to entertaining. You want to have a well-stocked kitchen and bar so that you have all the necessary platters and serving equipment on hand to host with confidence.

We suggest keeping with a white color scheme. It's a blank canvas for you to add color, pattern, and festivity through the use of flowers or smaller pieces like napkins, charger plates, or other décor. White linens are especially useful because they can be bleached to remove stains.

And we suggest buying everything in sets of 12 so you have enough to host small, medium, and large groups. Even if you find yourself hosting larger groups only a handful of times, it's still worth having a set of 12 on hand. Accidents happen, and knowing you have backup flatware and glassware in case something breaks or chips will give you peace of mind. You don't want to stress yourself out by running around at the last minute to find a matching plate because one of yours is chipped!

If you don't have the space or budget for a full set of 12, you can get by on a set of 8 (for families) or even 6 (for couples), using the logic that you generally have enough for the maximum number of guests you would host, then a couple of extra sets as backup.

FLATWARE

NOTE *Don't wash sterling silver cutlery in the dishwasher. Keep your pieces shiny by wiping them with a damp cloth dipped in a mixture of hot water and baking soda or white vinegar. Rinse under warm water and dry with a soft cloth.*

EXTRAVAGANT

12 sets of the best sterling silver flatware you can afford. Use them daily to make every day an occasion!

- Salad fork.
- Dinner fork.
- Knife.
- Dinner spoon.
- Dessert spoon.
- Optional: steak knife.

EVERYDAY

12 sets of stainless steel or other silver-colored flatware.

- Salad fork.
- Dinner fork.
- Knife.
- Dinner spoon.
- Dessert spoon.
- Optional: steak knife.

PLATEWARE

EXTRAVAGANT

12 white fine china matching plates for a 3-course meal.

- Dinner plate.
- Dessert plate.
- Side plate.
- Optional: pasta plate.
- Optional: soup bowl.

EVERYDAY

12 matching plates for a 3-course meal (ceramic, tempered glass, or other).

- Dinner plate.
- Dessert plate.
- Side plate.
- Optional: pasta plate.
- Optional: soup bowl.

LINEN

EXTRAVAGANT

Crisp white linen tablecloth and 12 white place mats. Purchase ones that can be easily wiped down or washed and ironed flat.

- 12 matching white linen dinner napkins. Even if your table can only fit 4 guests, you will always need extra napkins, and they'll come in handy if you're hosting a buffet.
- 12 (minimum) matching linen cocktail napkins, monogrammed.

EVERYDAY

Crisp white cotton tablecloth, 12 white place mats. Look for ones that can be easily wiped down or washed and ironed flat.

- 12 white cotton/cloth dinner napkins or durable paper napkins.
- Package of white cocktail napkins or durable paper napkins.

NOTE *We love monogramming. It's a small upfront investment, but it can be passed down from generation to generation while also adding that extra level of personalization.*

GLASSWARE

EXTRAVAGANT

- 14 crystal water glasses.
- 28 crystal wine glasses (14 red wine glasses, 14 white wine glasses).
- 14 crystal champagne flutes or coupes.
- 14 crystal cocktail glasses.
- 14 crystal shot glasses.

EVERYDAY

- 24 stemless wine glasses—they're chic, modern, and multipurpose. They can be used for red and white wine, water, and cocktails.
- 12 glass champagne flutes.
- 12 glass shot glasses.

NOTE *If you're investing in high-end crystal, we recommend getting a set of 12 plus 2 extra of each glass. Eventually a couple will break, and it saves you trying to source out single glasses down the road to keep your set of 12 complete.*

ACCENTS, EXTRAS + MORE

EXTRAVAGANT

- 12 candlesticks.
- 3 to 5 crystal or silver flower vases in various shapes, sizes, and heights.
- 2 (1 for each end of the table) matching salt + pepper shakers or silver bowls with spoons.

EVERYDAY

- 12 votive holders and tea lights (wax or LED).
- 3 to 5 glass vases in varying shapes, sizes, and heights.
- 2 (1 for each end of the table) salt + pepper shakers.

SEB SAYS *When it comes to buying platters for serving canapés, always check your inventory before you shop to see what will complement your current pieces. Instead of making random purchases, build your inventory in a way that will let you mix and match.*

SERVING TOOLS

When it comes to building your tableware essentials, consider how you most often entertain and how much space you have. When we started hosting, as a young couple living in a small apartment, we had to get creative. We found pieces like small bowls that were great for our morning cereal but could also double as serving vessels for mixed nuts or chips for cocktail parties. When our entertaining style moved towards larger groups with seated meals and buffets, we began adding to our entertaining arsenal but never stopped considering how items could be used in different and interesting ways. The list below might seem lengthy but you don't need to buy everything at once. Start with what you expect to use the most and then add as you need.

SERVING ESSENTIALS FOR THE TABLE

- 12 mini forks for hors d'oeuvres.
- 12 appetizer/mini plates for hors d'oeuvres.
- 2 wooden platters for charcuterie platters or grilled meat.
- 3 to 5 very small bowls for dips, jams, jellies, or discarded olive pits.
- 2 to 3 medium bowls for crackers, chips, olives, etc.
- Silver glass or shot glass for toothpicks.
- 1 set of cheese knives.
- An assortment of platters to serve food. Stick with a single shape (round, oval, square, rectangular) and a single color, preferably white. Have at least 2 small, 2 medium, and 2 large. You can never have too many!
- 1 large salad bowl, wood or white.
- 1 large cake stand.
- 1 small cake stand. Large and small cake stands can be stacked to create a canapé tower, seafood tower, etc.
- 2 serving trays in silver or white for serving drinks and transporting platters or canapés.
- 1–2 clear acrylic serving dishes as outdoor alternatives to the silver or white trays.
- 2–3 sets of large serving spoons and forks.

SERVING ESSENTIALS FOR THE BAR

We love getting creative behind the bar. You'll see in this book that we greet our guests with a signature welcome cocktail at almost every party we host. It's slightly more elevated than wine and sets the party off on a good note. We like to be especially creative with our welcome cocktails and give our guests something unexpected and new to try.

In addition to the items listed below, we have a few essential accompaniments we keep on hand and available for guests to use: a small bowl filled with freshly cut lemon and lime wedges—not only are they good additions to many aperitifs and digestifs, but they can also be used to flavor water and sodas—and small dishes filled with salt and sugar to rim glasses.

MUST-HAVES

- Wine opener: you can buy fancy electric ones, but a simple manual one does the trick and is easier to store.
- Bottle opener.
- Pitcher, punch bowl, or drink dispenser for batched cocktails.
- Tray for drinks display or glasses, large enough to fit at least 6 glasses.
- Wine bucket.
- Martini shaker.
- Martini strainer.
- Jigger.
- Coasters.

NICE-TO-HAVES

- At least 2 glass wine decanters, 1 for red and 1 for white.
- Large wine bucket that holds at least 3 bottles.
- Ice bucket with tongs or a spoon.
- Cocktail mixing spoon (for mixing individual and batched drinks).
- Cocktail picks/stir sticks for garnishes like olives, etc.
- Muddler.

STOCK-ING THE BAR

We keep a few specific things in our home bar at all times. They make it easier to entertain at a moment's notice and allow us to serve a variety of beverages depending on our guests' tastes. There are many, many spirits and liqueurs out there, so we encourage you to tweak this list to reflect what you serve most often. For example, if you aren't big beer drinkers, only keep one or two varieties on hand.

Since we're serial entertainers, we invested in a wine fridge. The glass front makes it easy for us to see what we're low on. We like to organize our wines by first separating reds from whites and rosés, then by price (so Sheila knows what is for daily drinking versus special dinners), then by region and varietal, so our chosen wine pairs best with our menu. Like we said, preparation is key to stress-free entertaining!

WINES + BEERS

Try to offer both light-bodied and heavy-bodied wines to accommodate various palates. We like to have two reds and two whites on hand for every occasion. We'll choose a Californian pinot noir or a merlot for the lighter-bodied reds, and a full-bodied cabernet sauvignon for the heavy-bodied one. When it comes to whites, we like crisp, refreshing varietals like pinot grigio and chablis, but we often incorporate a fruitier sauvignon blanc or full-bodied buttery chardonnay. When it comes to sparkling, we generally use prosecco for everyday occasions or mixing and splurge on champagne for special occasions. Anyone who knows us knows that when it comes to rosé, we are traditionalists, opting for pale rosés from southern France.

Sometimes we also add a port wine, sherry, or moscato to match a specific course we are serving, like poached pears for dessert.

For beers, lagers are usually the most crowd-pleasing. If your guests enjoy beer, consider stocking a variety of craft beers (e.g., pale ales, stouts, etc., and even some ciders, which are quite popular these days). Be mindful when serving beers, as they can make or break an eating experience. That's why we recommend lagers. They complement most dishes well.

SPIRITS

Vodka, gin, and rum have always been considered essential bar spirits, but with the popularity of specialty cocktails, we keep tequila, whiskey, and bourbon on hand as well.

- Vodka.
- Gin.
- Rum.
- Tequila.
- Whiskey or bourbon.
- Scotch (blended or single malt).
- Brandy or cognac.

LIQUEURS

Stock your liqueurs based on the cocktails you're likely to be creating. If you're testing out a new drink, look for a small bottle (375 ml) before committing to a full-size one. There's nothing worse than having tons of unused liqueurs cluttering up your cabinet. Here are the liqueurs that we come back to again and again:

- Aperol or Campari.
- Amaretto.
- Kahlúa (coffee liqueur).
- Irish cream.
- Triple sec.
- Crème de cassis or chambord.
- Chartreuse.
- Limoncello.
- Maraschino.
- St. Germain.
- Bitters (grapefruit, orange, berry).
- Vermouth (dry and sweet).

MIX-INS

We like to have a variety of mixers that can be enjoyed with your favorite alcohol or on their own as a non-alcoholic beverage.

- Tonic water.
- Sparkling water/club soda.
- Fresh lemon juice.
- Unsweetened cranberry juice.
- Lemonade.
- Grapefruit juice.
- Grenadine.
- Coke/Diet Coke.
- Sprite.

GARNISHES

Garnishes should always include lemons and limes. The extra ingredients can be adjusted based on the cocktails being served and their recipes.

- Lemon wedges.
- Lime wedges.
- Orange slices.
- Maraschino cherries.
- Green olives.
- Mint leaves.
- Edible flowers.

SIMPLE SYRUP RECIPE

In a saucepan over medium-low heat, stir together equal volumes of sugar and water until the sugar is dissolved and the mixture comes to a boil. Let cool and store in a glass jar in the fridge for up to 1 week.

GRENADINE RECIPE

In a saucepan over medium heat, stir together 1 cup pomegranate juice and 1 cup sugar until the sugar is dissolved. Stir in 1 tsp lemon juice. Let cool. Store in a glass jar in the fridge for up to 4 weeks.

HOW TO BUILD A SELF-SERVE BAR

We use self-serve bars at many of our parties. Whether we're hosting a casual Sunday brunch, a mixed grill barbecue, or a more formal cocktail hour, we find them a stress-free way to present drinks to our guests. With a self-serve bar, you don't have to worry about running around and making sure your guests' glasses are always full, and you can spend more time with your guests. Self-serve drink stations can be set up quickly and don't need any specialty liquors or garnishes, which makes them perfect for impromptu get-togethers. We've come up with a few key ideas to get you setting up a self-serve bar in no time.

LOCATION

Set up your self-serve bar somewhere central. Keep in mind that guests tend to congregate wherever the drinks are, so make sure it's not blocking any seating or food. We typically set ours up at the end of a buffet bar or on its own on a small table set against one wall.

SETUP + EQUIPMENT

Set up your drink bar in the way a guest would make their drink. That means glasses first, then alcohol, mix-ins (juice, soda, etc.), and garnishes. There's no right or wrong way to set up the bar, but we like to place the glasses on a small tray and place the alcohol in an ice bucket (except red wine, of course). Right beside the alcohol we have the mix-ins in glass pitchers. You can also serve these on ice but it's not essential. At the end of the bar we place the garnishes in small bowls alongside some cocktail napkins and stir sticks.

To set up a self-serve drink bar you'll need:

- A large tray, place mat, or cutting board to ground the drink station.
- A small tray for the glasses.
- Glasses.
- 2 large buckets: 1 filled with ice to use in the drinks and 1 filled with ice to hold the cold drinks.
- At least 3 pitchers for the mix-ins.
- At least 3 small bowls for the garnishes.
- Cocktail napkins.
- Small tongs or toothpicks for picking up the garnishes.
- Small spoons or stir sticks for guests to mix their drinks.

THE DRINKS

Self-serve bars should not require your guests to become mixologists. Keep it simple with 1 to 3 alcohol options, 3 mix-in options, and 3 garnishes. Here are some of our favorites:

ALCOHOL

- Champagne.
- Vodka.
- Tequila.
- White wine.

MIX-IN

- Orange juice.
- Cranberry juice.
- Grapefruit juice.
- Lemonade.
- Soda water.

GARNISH (SERVED FROZEN)

- Sliced grapefruit.
- Sliced lemon.
- Sliced lime.
- Cut pineapple.
- Cherries.
- Strawberries.
- Blueberries.
- Blackberries.

Some of our favorite combinations to make from the self-serve bar are:

- Vodka + lemonade + lemon slice
- Tequila + orange juice + lime slice
- White wine + soda water + blackberry garnish
- Vodka + soda water + cranberry juice + frozen cherry
- Champagne + grapefruit juice + pineapple

CHAR-
CUTERIE
+
CHEESE
BOARD
BASICS

While charcuterie technically refers to smoked, cured, or cooked meats, it is more often used these days to describe a complete platter of meats, cheeses, fruits, crackers, and spreads. Knowing how to build a charcuterie board is a key skill when it comes to entertaining. With a quick trip to the deli and a few pantry staples, you can create a charcuterie board that is sure to impress your guests. They can be made in advance and kept in the fridge, but they're easy enough to whip together at a moment's notice for an impromptu get-together with neighbors. With the wide variety of items you can include, a charcuterie board is the perfect grazing dish for a cocktail party, before a seated meal, or even as a first course for a summer luncheon in the garden.

There is no wrong way to build a charcuterie platter. The most important factor is to make sure that everything on your board can sit at room temperature. Charcuterie boards are meant to be enjoyed slowly, so choose items that keep fresh for at least a few hours. Here are a few other pointers we like to follow when assembling our charcuterie platters.

- Start with a large, flat platter. Marble slabs, trays, and cutting boards are perfect. You do not want to use a platter with any sloping, as it will make it difficult to display your charcuterie.

- For the cheese, try to accommodate as many palates as possible. Not everyone loves soft cheeses like brie or camembert, so include something like a white cheddar or a crumbled parmigiano-reggiano as well. Here is a quick guide you can follow when it comes to choosing cheeses for your charcuterie board. Choose at least one from each category and estimate that each person will consume about 5 ounces of cheese in total.

- **AGED** Cheddar, Gruyère, Gouda.
- **BLUE** Maytag, Stilton.
- **HARD** Manchego, Parmigiano-Reggiano, Beemster, Emmental.
- **SOFT** Brie, Camembert, Bourgogne.

- Remove your cheeses from the fridge at least 1 hour before your guests arrive. Cheese is much more flavorful once it reaches room temperature! Wrap extras and leftovers in parchment or wax paper followed by plastic wrap or a plastic bag, or for a more environmentally-friendly option, use a reusable container into which you can place several wrapped cheeses of the same variety.

- Moving onto the meats, a spicy Genoa salami is our favorite, but for those with a less adventurous palate, a simple prosciutto is perfect.

- Always pair your cheeses with a variety of accompaniments like olives or olive tapenade, cornichons, dried and fresh fruits, nuts, jellies, honeys, and balsamic vinegar or glazes, or even dark chocolate. It's also important to have an

assortment of bread and crackers, such as fresh baguette, water crackers, gluten-free crackers, savory shortbreads, and artisan crisps. Have fun with the flavors and textures and don't be afraid to add something unexpected. Our go-to is honey served right off the honeycomb, since most people likely won't have seen this before, but nowadays you can buy it at most high-end grocery stores.

· When it comes to assembling your board, build the components up to different heights rather than laying all the food flat. You can do this by using differently shaped cheeses, pleating over or rolling your cured meats for texture, building small bundles of grapes still on the stem, or even adding mini bowls for your condiments. We recommend starting with your cheese and meat, since they'll likely take up the most space on your board, and then filling in the space with the accompaniments, being careful to not put similar colors side by side or all the meat in one section and all the fruit in another. We also like to put as much on the platter as possible, including the jellies and honeycomb. It's also helpful to slice some of the cheeses ahead of time to make it easy for your guests to serve themselves. Not everyone likes to be the first to cut into the cheese!

Use this checklist to make sure you have every element covered on your board or to give you some ideas for new flavors to include.

· **SALTY** Salted nuts, chips.
· **TANGY** Olives, cornichons, artichoke hearts, grainy or smooth Dijon mustard.
· **FRESH** Fresh figs, melon, radishes.
· **NUTTY** Almonds, pistachios, walnuts.

· **SWEET** Dried fruit, jams, honey, roasted red peppers.
· **CRUNCHY** Crackers, toasted baguette.
· **SOMETHING UNEXPECTED** European-style butter, honeycomb, dark chocolate.

PARTY MATH

4-6 PEOPLE

ICE
6 lb

GARNISHES (LEMONS AND LIMES)
3 of each

CANAPÉS
4 to 6 varieties,
6 to 8 pieces of each

CHEESES (DOMESTIC + INTERNATIONIAL)
2 to 3 varieties

SPRING + SUMMER
RED WINE / WHITE WINE / ROSÉ
1-2 bottles / 2 bottles / 2 bottles

FALL + WINTER
RED WINE / WHITE WINE / ROSÉ
2 bottles / 2 bottles / none

BEER
12 bottles

BASIC SPIRITS
VODKA, GIN, TEQUILA, RYE OR RUM
1 bottle of each

POP
COKE, DIET COKE, GINGER ALE (355 ML CANS)
2 cans of each

JUICE
CRANBERRY, ORANGE, GRAPEFRUIT (1 LITRE)
1 bottle of each

SODA/TONIC (355 ML. CANS)
4 soda, 2 tonic

7-10 PEOPLE

ICE
10 lb

GARNISHES (LEMONS AND LIMES)
4 of each

CANAPÉS
8 varieties,
6 to 8 pieces of each

CHEESES (DOMESTIC + INTERNATIONIAL)
3 to 4 varieties

SPRING + SUMMER
RED WINE / WHITE WINE / ROSÉ
3 bottles / 3 bottles / 3 bottles

FALL + WINTER
RED WINE / WHITE WINE / ROSÉ
4 bottles / 3 bottles / none

BEER
18 bottles

BASIC SPIRITS
VODKA, GIN, TEQUILA, RYE OR RUM
1 bottle of each

POP
COKE, DIET COKE, GINGER ALE (355 ML CANS)
3 cans of each

JUICE
CRANBERRY, ORANGE, GRAPEFRUIT (1 LITRE)
1 bottle of each

SODA/TONIC (355 ML. CANS)
6 soda, 3 tonic

10–14 PEOPLE

ICE
15 lb

GARNISHES (LEMONS AND LIMES)
5 of each

CANAPÉS
8 varieties,
10 pieces of each

CHEESES (DOMESTIC + INTERNATIONIAL)
6 varieties

SPRING + SUMMER
RED WINE / WHITE WINE / ROSÉ
4 bottles / 4 bottles / 4-5 bottles

FALL + WINTER
RED WINE / WHITE WINE / ROSÉ
6 bottles / 6 bottles / none

BEER
24 bottles

BASIC SPIRITS
VODKA, GIN, TEQUILA, RYE OR RUM
2 bottles of each

POP
COKE, DIET COKE, GINGER ALE (355 ML CANS)
4 cans of each

JUICE
CRANBERRY, ORANGE, GRAPEFRUIT (1 LITRE)
1 bottle of each

SODA/TONIC (355 ML CANS)
8 soda, 4 tonic

24 PEOPLE

ICE
25 lb

GARNISHES (LEMONS AND LIMES)
8 of each

CANAPÉS
8-10 varieties,
12-14 pieces of each

CHEESES (DOMESTIC + INTERNATIONIAL)
6 varieties (2 of each)

SPRING + SUMMER
RED WINE / WHITE WINE / ROSÉ
6 bottles / 8 bottles / 10-12 bottles

FALL + WINTER
RED WINE / WHITE WINE / ROSÉ
8-10 bottles / 8-10 bottles / none

BEER
36 bottles

BASIC SPIRITS
VODKA, GIN, TEQUILA, RYE OR RUM
3 bottles of each

POP
COKE, DIET COKE, GINGER ALE (355 ML CANS)
8 cans of each

JUICE
CRANBERRY, ORANGE, GRAPEFRUIT (1 LITRE)
2 bottles of each

SODA/TONIC (355 ML CANS)
12 soda, 6 tonic

Many people think that hosting requires lots of work, time, and effort, but it doesn't have to be like that. The trick is to start small, get comfortable, and then slowly add elements as you become more at ease with hosting.

Casual or impromptu get-togethers account for most of the entertaining we do, and often they are just as appreciated by our guests as a five-course meal. We don't let a hectic schedule keep us from indulging in our love for gathering together friends and family—and neither should you!

Known in some quarters as a cinq à sept in homage to the typical cocktail hours of 5:00 pm to 7:00 pm in France, a cocktail party is a fun and simple way of socializing without the pressure of preparing a full dinner. As such, it's especially well-suited to those who may be new to entertaining or aren't yet ready to pull out all the stops.

For us, cocktail parties often make for our most memorable evenings, with lots of laughter and great conversation, since they let you mingle with different people throughout the evening, instead of only chatting with the people sitting near you at the table.

One of the best things about a cocktail party is that you can adjust your menu based on how many people you're accommodating. From the backyard to the kitchen, no formal seating is required, and party crashing should be encouraged. A couple of extra guests won't add any work. We like to tell people that our door only opens inwards!

We like to invite guests who don't know each other, as cocktail parties are a great way to make new friends. When you're making introductions, try to slip in a comment or two about something your guests have in common to help the conversation flow.

COCKTAIL PARTY 101

1

SIMPLE ENTER-TAINING

SEB SAYS

Signature cocktails are fun, chic, and unexpected. I find serving my guests a special cocktail as they walk through the door is a great way to make them feel welcomed.

SETTING

As we said, you can host a cocktail party in almost any area of your home. Unlike at a traditional seated dinner, guests can mingle and move around as they enjoy their cocktails and canapés. Separate the bar from the food to help avoid overcrowding and to encourage movement and flow.

Your cocktail party doesn't need to be a formal occasion, which means you can scale back on the décor. More often than not, small floral arrangements and votive candles strategically placed throughout your home will be enough to add a touch of elegance, and the glow of candles later in the evening will enhance the mood. For florals, you can choose simple, inexpensive greens with perhaps a single stem or two for a bit of color.

A great way to further enhance the ambience of your cocktail party is to choose the right music. Look for a simple playlist with a mix of old-time classics and songs everyone is likely to know, and play it at a level that's *just right* to have in the background. Avoid playing the music too loudly, as it can force guests to talk over one another.

Since you'll be offering a variety of canapés throughout your cocktail party, we recommend using a few classic platters or trays to serve your food. Set the canapé trays up on your kitchen counter, island, coffee table, or any other surface that feels inviting for your guests. If you're entertaining in a large space, try spreading the canapés out so your guests always have something to eat nearby.

SHEILA SAYS

Choosing the right playlist can be a daunting task, but I've got you covered. Search "Seb and Sheila" on mixcloud.com to listen to one of my Dinner Series Playlists!

SEB SAYS *For added variety or for larger cocktail parties, a great addition to the canapé list below is a quality charcuterie board. For tips on how to assemble the perfect charcuterie board, see pages 14-15.*

One of the most important things to consider when deciding on the canapé menu for your cocktail party is variety. It's a fine line to walk, but the best cocktail parties are those with a canapé selection that appeals to a wide range of tastes.

Although we offer recipes for several different canapés in this chapter, consider how many people you're hosting before you decide to add or omit any dishes. If you're having trouble determining portions, feel free to consult the party math table (pages 16–17) for help with estimating how many canapés and drinks you'll need per guest.

COURSES

Since a cocktail party is all about mingling and moving around, we like to have the canapés mostly prepared and ready to serve before our guests arrive. For this specific menu, we've selected all room-temperature items that can be prepared ahead of time so your attention can be turned to hosting instead of spending the entire night in the kitchen.

The first canapé we are serving is Prosciutto-Wrapped Asparagus: blanched asparagus wrapped with prosciutto and topped with olive oil and grated parmigiano-reggiano cheese. This simple and light canapé always ends up being devoured early on in the evening. Some people may prefer wrapping the asparagus in bunches of two or three stems, but since we're serving them as finger foods, we recommend wrapping them individually.

Filled with a simple goat cheese mixture, and topped with toasted nuts and honey, our Chèvre Endive Cups are packed with delicious flavors that are sure to have your guests reaching for more. What we also love about this canapé is how the endive is easy to handle and works like a spoon.

Another delicious canapé option is Crab Cucumber Cups: hollowed-out cucumbers filled with crab salad. This recipe might take a bit more prep than the endive cups, but the result is definitely worth the few extra minutes!

Next, we like to serve Stuffed Onion Cups: onions filled with sweet green peas and topped with salty feta. This recipe makes for a beautiful and healthy dish that always seems to be among the first platters gone. For some added beauty, try using red onions and marinating them in vinegar once you've separated them into cups! This will brighten the color of the onion and allow it to contrast beautifully against the green peas.

WHAT'S ON THE MENU

TIP

If you need to substitute walnuts because of a nut allergy for another crunchy topping in your Chèvre Endive Cups, try using pumpkin or sunflower seeds. Or, if you're up for a little more work, fry thinly sliced shallots in vegetable or olive oil until golden and drain on a paper towel to crisp up before using. The extra work will be worth it, we promise!

One bite-sized item that is not only delicious but also beautiful is a Bacon-Wrapped Pretzel: a pretzel rod wrapped with bacon and seasonings. Instead of laying the bacon-wrapped sticks on a plate like you would for the asparagus, we like to serve them in silver cups with a stem of fresh rosemary as garnish.

And for something slightly different, we've taken the idea of classic bruschetta, which everyone loves, and turned it into a self-serve DIY Bruschetta Bar. This format allows guests to choose between three toppings in the ultimate bruschetta-style self-serve platter. Whether your guests stick to just one topping or mix multiple styles, they will certainly be impressed with the clever way you turned a classic canapé into a completely customizable one.

WHAT'S ON THE BAR

While the canapés are important, it goes without saying that the main focus of your cocktail party should, of course, be the cocktails! If you're like us and you love trying something new, treat your cocktail party as an opportunity to experiment with some fun new combinations.

The easiest way to encourage your guests to stray from their typical cocktail of choice is by offering them a welcome cocktail as they walk through the door. We like to suggest something light and charming, like a Grapefruit Sparkler Cocktail. It's easy to make and it requires just a few ingredients: simply add a sugar cube to a champagne flute along with a few dashes of bitters. When your guests arrive, pour champagne or prosecco into the flute and watch the sugar cube fizz for that "wow" factor. A brut champagne tends to work best for this.

On top of the welcome cocktail, we like to suggest offering two specialty cocktails. The first is a Batched Southern Lemonade. Served in either a carafe or a punch bowl, this whiskey-based cocktail is best served alongside a small bowl of lemon wedges for garnish. Unlike most cocktails, which should be prepared à la minute, this one should be prepared and left to chill in the fridge for about 1 hour before serving.

The second specialty cocktail we like to offer can be mixed right in front of your guests. For this drink, all you'll need is chambord liqueur, white wine, soda, and some blackberries. Like the Batched Southern Lemonade, a Chambord Spritz can be prepared as a batch.

TIP

For your less adventurous guests, have a few basic wines and liquors available should they not want to experiment with specialty cocktails.

SEB SAYS

Try using tiered trays to present your canapés for an interesting alternative to platters that will grab your guests' attention. Don't have tiered trays? No problem. Just stack two sizes of cake stands or use plates separated with short glasses to make your own.

COCKTAIL PARTY 101

COCKTAILS

GRAPEFRUIT SPARKLER COCKTAIL (P30)

BATCHED SOUTHERN LEMONADE (P30)

CHAMBORD SPRITZ (P31)

CANAPÉS

PROSCIUTTO-WRAPPED ASPARAGUS (P34)

BACON-WRAPPED PRETZELS (P34)

CHÈVRE ENDIVE CUPS (P35)

CRAB CUCUMBER CUPS (P35)

STUFFED ONION CUPS (P36)

BRUSCHETTA BAR (P39)

SHEILA SAYS

If you choose too many complex cocktails, you'll end up bartending all night. I like to mix up our offerings with some batched cocktails that are easy to serve and other cocktails with simple ingredients that are easy for our guests to mix themselves.

PARTY COUNTDOWN:

COCKTAIL PARTY 101

3 THREE DAYS BEFORE

○ Send a reminder email or text to your guests with details about the evening.

○ Plan your menu to make sure you have enough for your guests to eat and drink.

○ Make your grocery and alcohol list.

○ Check your platter and bar inventory and decide what platters you will use for each canapé.

○ Check your bar to make sure you have enough glasses and pitchers for your cocktails and batched drinks. The last thing you want to have to do during your cocktail party is wash glasses!

2 TWO DAYS BEFORE

○ Grocery shop and stock up at the liquor store.

○ Plan where you'll set up your canapé platters, candles, and florals.

Omit a second batched cocktail or serve two batched.

Instead of creating your own flower arrangements, buy several small prepared arrangements.

1 THE DAY BEFORE

- ◯ Buy flowers, trim them, and place them in water overnight.

- ◯ Blanch the asparagus and refrigerate in an airtight container.

- ◯ Prepare the crab mixture for the cucumber cups and refrigerate in an airtight container.

- ◯ Prepare the pea mixture for the onion cups and refrigerate in an airtight container.

0 THE DAY OF

- ◯ Prepare the floral arrangements.

- ◯ Wrap the asparagus with the prosciutto.

- ◯ Prepare the bacon-wrapped pretzels.

- ◯ Assemble the endive cups.

- ◯ Prepare the onion cups.

- ◯ Prepare the toppings for the bruschetta bar.

GRAPEFRUIT SPARKLER COCKTAIL

COCKTAILS

GRAPEFRUIT SPARKLER COCKTAIL

yield: makes 1 cocktail · prep time: 5 minutes

Ingredients
1 sugar cube
1 dash grapefruit or other bitters
Prosecco, champagne, or sparkling wine
1 gooseberry, for garnish

Method
Soak the sugar cube in the bitters and then drop it into a champagne flute.

Fill the flute with prosecco.

Make a small slice in the bottom of the gooseberry and place it on the rim of the flute to garnish.

TIP

Consider setting up a mini cocktail station near your front entrance with a tray of flutes, a small bowl of sugar cubes, a little bottle of bitters, and a bottle of prosecco on ice. Mixing this cocktail takes only a few seconds and provides some entertainment as guests arrive.

BATCHED SOUTHERN LEMONADE

yield: makes 6–8 cocktails · prep time: 10 minutes

Ingredients
8 oz Tennessee whiskey (we like Jack Daniel's)
4 oz triple sec
½ cup lemon juice (3–4 lemons)
1½ cups lemonade
16 lemon slices

Method
Combine the whiskey, triple sec, lemon juice, lemonade, and 8 of the lemon slices in a large pitcher. Chill in the fridge for at least 1 hour before your guests are due, or up to overnight.

Fill rocks glasses with ice, then pour the lemonade overtop. Garnish each glass with a lemon slice.

CHAMBORD SPRITZ

yield: makes 1 cocktail · prep time: 2 minutes

Ingredients

4 oz dry white wine
1½ oz chambord liqueur
Soda water
2 blackberries, for garnish

Method

Fill a large wine glass or tumbler with ice. Add the wine, then the chambord. Top with soda and stir with a spoon. Garnish with the blackberries.

TIP

When you're making batched cocktails that use soda water or other non-alcoholic components, keep them separated so guests can control the strength of their drinks.

PROSCIUTTO-
WRAPPED
ASPARAGUS

BACON-WRAPPED
PRETZELS

STUFFED ONION CUPS,
CRAB CUCUMBER CUPS,
CHÈVRE ENDIVE CUPS

CANAPÉS

PROSCIUTTO-WRAPPED ASPARAGUS

yield: serves 6–8 · prep time: 10 minutes · cook time: 5 minutes

Ingredients

12 asparagus spears
12 slices prosciutto
Olive oil, for garnish
Balsamic glaze, for garnish
Shaved parmigiano-reggiano, for garnish

Method

Wash the asparagus. Snap off and remove the tough ends.

Bring a large pot of salted water to a boil over high heat and prepare an ice bath. Place the asparagus in the boiling water and cook until it turns bright green, 2–3 minutes. Immediately transfer the asparagus to the ice bath (or rinse them in a colander under cold water if you prefer). Set aside to cool. (If you're cooking ahead, refrigerate them overnight.)

Wrap 1 slice of prosciutto around each cooled asparagus spear. Depending on the size of prosciutto and thickness of the asparagus, you may be able to cut a prosciutto slice lengthwise in half and wrap two spears.

Serve on a platter and garnish with oil, balsamic glaze, and parmigiano-reggiano.

BACON-WRAPPED PRETZELS

yield: serves 6–8 · prep time: 20 minutes + 20–30 minutes to cool · cook time: 25 minutes

Ingredients

¾ lb thin-cut bacon (about 12 slices)
1 cup packed brown sugar
3 Tbsp chili powder
½ tsp sea salt
⅛ tsp cayenne pepper
12 (each about 6 inches long) pretzel rods
1 rosemary sprig, for garnish

Method

Remove the bacon from the fridge to come to room temperature.

Preheat the oven to 350°F. Line a baking sheet with parchment paper, place a wire rack on top, and spray the rack and the parchment paper generously with cooking spray.

In a large baking tray or shallow bowl, mix together the sugar, chili powder, salt, and cayenne pepper.

Dredge both sides of 1 slice of bacon in the seasoning, carefully wrap it around the entire length of 1 pretzel, and place it on the wire rack. Repeat with the remaining bacon and pretzels.

Bake the pretzels until crisp, 20–25 minutes. When they come out of the oven, they'll be limp and soft to the touch. Let them cool completely on the wire rack, 20–30 minutes, until they harden.

Serve in a galvanized pail or cup with the rosemary for garnish.

CHÈVRE ENDIVE CUPS

yield: serves 6–8 · prep time: 20 minutes · cook time: 5 minutes

Ingredients
½ cup walnut halves
3 full endives
10½ oz chèvre
2 Tbsp whipping (36%) cream
½ tsp coarse sea salt
½ tsp black pepper
½ green apple, peeled
½ lemon, juice of
4 tsp honey

Method
Preheat the oven to 325°F.

Place the walnuts on a baking tray and bake until lightly toasted, 4–5 minutes, mixing halfway through to prevent browning. Set aside to cool, then chop into small pieces.

Cut the base from the endive heads to release the leaves from the root. Carefully separate the leaves and gently wipe them with a clean dish cloth or paper towel to remove any dirt. Set aside 12 of the larger leaves to use for the cups. Store the remaining leaves in an airtight container in the fridge for another use.

In a medium bowl and using a handheld mixer, whip together the cheese, cream, salt, and pepper until fluffy, about 5 minutes. Set aside.

Mince the apple and place it in a small bowl with the lemon juice to prevent browning.

Arrange the endive cups on your serving platter. Fill each cup with about 1 Tbsp of the goat cheese mixture, drizzle with some honey, and top with toasted walnuts, diced apple, and a pinch of salt.

CRAB CUCUMBER CUPS

yield: serves 6–8 · prep time: 30 minutes

Ingredients
6 mini cucumbers
1½ cups crab meat, drained and diced
½ cup cream cheese, softened
1 shallot, finely minced
1 Tbsp chopped curly parsley
1 Tbsp chopped dill
1 Tbsp minced red bell pepper
½ cup low-fat sour cream
1 Tbsp lemon juice
1 tsp brown mustard
Sea salt and black pepper
6 chives, thinly sliced
Spanish paprika

Method
Cut the cucumbers into 1-inch rounds. Using a melon baller, small spoon, or paring knife, scoop out the center of each cucumber piece, without going all the way through the round, to remove the pulp and seeds (you want a slight base on each cucumber round). Place them on the serving platter.

In a medium bowl, mix together the crab meat, cream cheese, shallot, parsley, dill, bell pepper, sour cream, lemon juice, mustard, and salt and pepper to taste until fully combined.

Carefully scoop the crab mixture into each cucumber cup. Garnish with the chives and a pinch of paprika. Refrigerate for up to 30 minutes uncovered. If you're making this ahead of time, refrigerate the crab mixture, covered and separate from the cucumber cups, and assemble 30 minutes before serving.

STUFFED ONION CUPS

yield: serves 6–8 · prep time: 30 minutes · cook time: 15 minutes

Ingredients

3 small red onions or large shallots

1 cup apple cider vinegar

1 lb frozen and thawed peas

4 garlic cloves, divided

1½ tsp sea salt, divided

1 shallot

¼ cup + 1 tsp olive oil, divided

Black pepper

½ cup dry white wine

2 Tbsp chopped curly parsley

2 Tbsp chopped chives

6 fresh mint leaves + more for garnish

½ lemon, grated zest and juice of + more zest for garnish

Crumbled feta, for garnish

Method

Bring a large pot of water to a boil over high heat. Boil the onions whole, with their skins on, for 2–3 minutes. Drain and let cool.

Cut the root end off each onion and remove the skin. Slice the onions crosswise into ½-inch-thick rings. Separate the onion layers into cups. Set aside the medium-sized cups. The remaining onion cups can be refrigerated or frozen for another use.

In a medium stockpot, bring 8 cups of water and the vinegar to a boil. Prepare an ice bath.

Place the onion cups in the boiling water and cook until translucent, 3–4 minutes. Transfer to the ice bath, then set aside to dry on a clean kitchen towel. The vinegar will help them keep their bright color.

Brush a nonstick skillet with some oil, set it over high heat, and place the onions cut side down in the oil. Cook, without stirring or turning, until their edges develop a dark char, about 2–3 minutes. You may need to do this in batches to avoid overcrowding the pan.

In a medium stockpot set over medium heat, combine the peas, 2 of the garlic cloves, and 1 tsp salt. Fill with enough room-temperature water to cover the peas by 1 inch. Cook until the water comes to a boil and the peas turn bright green, 1–2 minutes. Discard the garlic, and then transfer the peas to the ice bath.

Roughly chop the shallot and the remaining 2 cloves of garlic. Sauté them in a large skillet over medium heat with the 1 tsp of oil until fragrant, about 1 minute. Season with the remaining ½ tsp of salt and pepper to taste. Add the wine and stir until the alcohol has evaporated, about 2 minutes.

Let cool slightly, then transfer to a blender with three-quarters of the peas, the remaining ¼ cup of oil, the parsley, chives, mint, and lemon zest and juice. Purée until smooth. Transfer to a bowl and fold in the remaining peas. Refrigerate until ready to serve.

Fill each onion cup with pea purée and garnish with more mint, lemon zest, and feta.

BRUSCHETTA BAR

yield: serves 6–8 of each canapé · prep time: 30 minutes + 30 minutes–overnight to rest · cook time: 20 minutes

Ingredients

CROSTINI
2 large baguettes
¼ cup olive oil

TOMATOES
3 medium on-the-vine tomatoes
½ pint cherry tomatoes
2 small garlic cloves
1½ Tbsp olive oil
4–6 large basil leaves, torn
1 oregano sprig, leaves only
¼ tsp sea salt
Black pepper

MUSHROOMS
3 small garlic cloves
2 Tbsp olive oil
1 lb mixed mushrooms
3 thyme sprigs
1 rosemary sprig
½ tsp sea salt
¼ tsp black pepper
1 Tbsp balsamic vinegar, optional
2 Tbsp chopped flat-leaf parsley

ZUCCHINIS
2 zucchinis
1½ Tbsp olive oil
½ lemon, juice of
1 Tbsp chopped basil
1 tsp chopped dill
¼ tsp sea salt
2 Tbsp shaved parmigiano-
  reggiano

Method

FOR THE CROSTINI
Preheat the oven to broil. Cut the baguettes into thin slices, about ¼-inch to ⅓-inch thick. You should get between 15 and 20 slices from a large baguette. Place the slices on a baking sheet and brush lightly with the oil. Broil, flipping once, until the slices are lightly toasted and golden brown, 5–10 minutes.

Remove from the oven and cool. If you're preparing the crostini more than 1–2 hours before the event, store in an airtight container to keep them crispy.

FOR THE TOMATOES
Cut the vine tomatoes into bite-sized pieces and quarter the cherry tomatoes. Crush the garlic with the heel of your hand or the flat edge of a knife so that it is flattened but still intact.

Place the tomatoes and garlic in a medium bowl and add the remaining tomato ingredients. Set aside for at least 1 hour for the flavors to amalgamate. Remove the garlic before serving.

FOR THE MUSHROOMS
Slightly crush the garlic with the heel of your hand or the flat edge of a knife so that it is flattened but still intact.

Heat the oil in a large skillet over medium heat. Add the garlic and fry until fragrant, about 30 seconds. Remove the garlic from the oil, reduce the heat to low, and add the mushrooms, thyme, rosemary, salt, and pepper. Cover and cook, stirring occasionally, until the mushrooms are soft, 7–9 minutes.

Add the balsamic and cook until all the liquid has evaporated, about 1 minute. Stir in the parsley, then remove from the heat and let cool slightly.

Pour the mushroom mixture onto a cutting board. Chop the mushrooms and garlic into bite-sized pieces.

FOR THE ZUCCHINIS
Using a vegetable peeler, peel the zucchinis to make ribbons, then roughly chop them into shorter lengths (1–2 inches long). Set aside in a medium bowl.

In a mason jar, whisk together the oil, lemon juice, basil, dill, and salt to make a vinaigrette.

Add the parmigiano-reggiano to the zucchini bowl, followed by the vinaigrette, and toss until completely coated. Set aside uncovered at room temperature for at least 30 minutes, or up to overnight in the fridge, covered, for the zucchini to soften and the flavors to amalgamate.

TO SERVE
Serve all the components alongside the toasted baguette slices.

All our friends and family know how much we value our time (and of course, meals) in the south of France and how these visits over the years have influenced our approach to entertaining. Our connection to France goes back to Seb's childhood, when he and his family would spend entire summers in his mother's native country.

Seb's mother grew up in Brittany, on the coast of the English Channel in the north of France—a place known for its amazing cuisine and fresh seafood. In her early twenties, she moved to Paris to study and work, and there she met Seb's father, who was a visiting economics post-graduate student from Canada. When he asked her to come back to Toronto with him, Seb's mother made him promise that they would return to France each year so she could keep her connection to her homeland, her friends, and her family.

Eventually, when Seb and his brother were born, his parents bought a small home in the south of France, where their family tradition evolved into spending the entire summer there and they became immersed in the lifestyle and culture that we now hold so dear. Seb's memories of these times will always be some of the fondest of his life. His mom's love of entertaining, hosting, and cooking was the cornerstone of their French experience.

Despite the many extraordinary meals we've enjoyed in France over the years, nothing satisfies our cravings for French cuisine quite like mussels do.

Some people only order mussels at a restaurant because of how intimidating the preparation seems, but if you use a simple recipe and straightforward ingredients, it isn't nearly as difficult as you might think. Most supermarkets have cleaned, ready-to-use mussels at the seafood counter. Ask for the mussels to be double-bagged and packed on ice so they stay cold until you can get them in your fridge.

When we're hosting a mussels dinner we like to keep appetizers to a minimum so our guests don't fill up before the main course. A few light, colorful canapés will help tide your guests over until the mussels are served. Though some people prefer to serve their salad course as an appetizer, we often adopt the traditionally European way and serve our salad course as a palate cleanser between the main course and dessert.

A MUSSELS DINNER

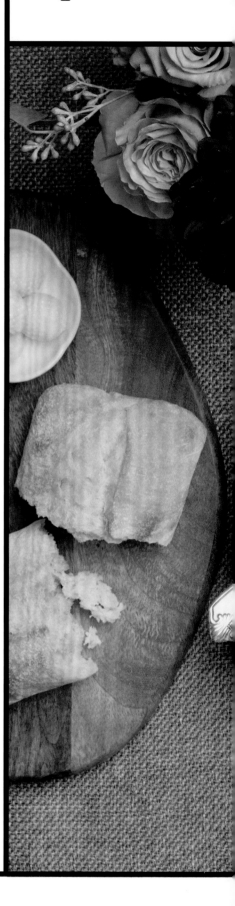

TIP *If you're having trouble finding a few small flower arrangements, purchase a large bouquet from the florist and divide it into smaller bouquets at home.*

SHEILA SAYS *If you don't have matching cutting boards, use mismatched ones. I typically preach consistency, but for this dinner, the mismatched element will work perfectly with the rustic theme.*

SETTING

Family-style meals like this one are all about comfort, so instead of going above and beyond to set an extravagant table, we like to set a simple, rustic table setting.

For a mussels dinner, we like to use wooden cutting boards instead of charger plates or serving platters. Not only does this add to the rustic theme, but it also alleviates the need for a tablecloth, as it gives the table some added depth and visual interest.

When you're setting the table for large groups it's important to plan well in advance and make sure that you leave some open space to help balance the table. Florals are one of the easiest ways to overcrowd your table, so for big dinners like this one we recommend having three or four small arrangements of flowers that you can position around the table with ease. We like incorporating rich colors like burgundies, dark reds, and dark greens to stay with the rustic theme.

To personalize our table, we add customized miniature baguettes wrapped in craft paper, and scatter small bowls of butter across the table. Along with being your guests' favorite social media shot of the night, mini baguettes will give your guests something to nibble on with every course. Whether guests use it to sop up all the sauce and delicious juices from the mussels or slather it with some salted butter, fresh baguette is always a crowd-pleaser.

As we mentioned earlier, in lieu of serving traditional appetizers, we like to begin our mussels dinner with a mixture of one-bite canapés. Some of our favorites are cucumber loonies, feta phyllo sticks, and radishes with butter and gourmet salt. Each of these European-inspired canapés can be prepared well ahead of time.

COURSES

As the canapés disappear, it's time for you and your guests to move to the table for the seated course. For tonight's main course, we'll be serving mussels and shrimp over pasta with a spicy arrabiata sauce.

One of the reasons we chose this course is that the recipe may be simple but the end result is very impressive. Pasta may seem pretty basic, but the mussels and shrimp take it up several levels. This recipe also lends itself to being modified as you get more comfortable with it. We use store-bought arrabiata sauce, but feel free to get creative with perhaps a basil-infused tomato sauce or whatever your go-to tomato-based sauce normally is.

Another great thing about this recipe is how it can be scaled up or down according to whether you're cooking for two or twenty, making it a dish that is sure to become a staple in your repertoire. We started cooking this when we were a young couple hosting only a few friends in our tiny loft, but it has served us just as well for family gatherings and other large dinners.

Given how hearty the main course is, we've opted to follow it up with a simple leafy salad tossed in a light dressing with only a few ingredients. This serves as the perfect palate cleanser and is ideal leading into our choice of dessert.

Lemon tiramisu is one of our favorite desserts to serve not only because of how fresh it is after a heavier meal, but also because it can be prepared ahead of time. The pasta course needs to be prepared and served à la minute, which will take you away from your guests and into the kitchen, but you can quickly serve the individual tiramisus straight from the fridge, so you'll be back with your guests in no time.

WHAT'S ON THE MENU

WHAT'S ON THE BAR

Mussels can sometimes be a tricky meal to pair cocktails with, so for this dinner we recommend offering two classic cocktails along with a variety of wines.

First up is a Boulevardier Cocktail. This is similar to a Negroni but it uses whiskey instead of gin. Easy to mix and serve, Boulevardiers are the perfect drink to enjoy before making the switch to wine, because although they are not over-powering, generally one before dinner is enough.

Another cocktail that pairs well with a mussels dinner is a Fernet-Branca Martini. For this cocktail all you need is gin, sweet vermouth, and Fernet-Branca. Fernet-Branca is a digestif, so it's generally served after a meal, but it works per-fectly in this recipe. To add a touch of sweetness, and to upgrade the look of this cocktail, we like to garnish it with a small orange twist.

We love using dinner parties to try out new wines, so while you might want to include a few of your favorites, try to include some new red or white varieties to broaden your choices. Keep in mind that you don't need to break the bank, as simple wines are best for this rustic meal.

A MUSSELS DINNER

COCKTAILS

BOULEVARDIER COCKTAIL (P52)

FERNET-BRANCA MARTINI (P52)

CANAPÉS

CUCUMBER LOONIES (P52)

PHYLLO CHEESE ROLLS (P53)

RADISHES WITH BUTTER + FLAVORED SALTS (P53)

FIRST COURSE

MUSSELS + SHRIMP WITH PASTA IN ARRABIATA SAUCE (P55)

SECOND COURSE

SIMPLE GREEN SALAD (P56)

DESSERT

LEMON TIRAMISU (P59)

PARTY COUNTDOWN:

A MUSSELS DINNER

3 THREE DAYS BEFORE

○ Send a reminder email or text to your guests with details about the evening.

○ Make your grocery and alcohol list. Make a special note of the specialty items like gourmet salts for the radishes.

2 TWO DAYS BEFORE

○ Make sure you have enough dishes and glasses for your guests.

○ Grocery shop (but leave the mussels until the day before or day of the dinner) and stock up at the liquor store.

TIME- SAVING TIPS

Scale back on the salts you offer with the radishes. Flaky Maldon salt or even kosher salt is fine.

Buy frozen par-baked baguettes that you can finish baking just before your guests arrive to save you a trip to the bakery the day of your dinner.

Buy frozen shrimp and keep them in your freezer. Just like the frozen baguettes, they make this meal easier to pull together any day!

Nix the cocktails. A few good bottles of wine alone are great accompaniments for this meal.

1 THE DAY BEFORE

○ Buy flowers, trim them, and place them in water overnight.

○ Buy the mussels and keep them on ice in the fridge (or, ideally, do this the morning of your party).

○ Buy the shrimp—either freshly poached or raw—and refrigerate them overnight.

○ Prepare the lemon tiramisus and refrigerate them overnight.

○ Prepare the filling for the phyllo sticks so all you'll have to do the day of the dinner is roll and bake them.

0 THE DAY OF

○ Prepare the floral arrangements and set the table.

○ Wrap the baguettes.

○ Prepare the cucumber loonies.

○ Prepare the phyllo sticks.

○ Assemble the radishes and butter.

BOULEVARDIER
COCKTAIL

FERNET-BRANCA
MARTINI

PHYLLO CHEESE
ROLLS

CUCUMBER
LOONIES

COCKTAILS +
SNACKS

BOULEVARDIER COCKTAIL

yield: makes 1 cocktail · prep time: 2 minutes

Ingredients
1½ oz bourbon whiskey
1 oz sweet or semi-sweet vermouth
1 oz Luxardo Bitter or Campari
Ice
Orange peel, for garnish

Method
Stir the bourbon, vermouth, and Luxardo Bitter together in a cocktail shaker. Strain over ice into an old-fashioned glass. Garnish with the orange peel.

FERNET-BRANCA MARTINI

yield: makes 1 cocktail · prep time: 2 minutes

Ingredients
1½ oz gin
1½ oz sweet vermouth
½ tsp Fernet-Branca
Orange twist, for garnish (see note)

Method
Stir the gin, sweet vermouth, and Fernet-Branca over ice in a cocktail shaker. Strain into a chilled martini glass. Garnish with an orange twist.

Note
To make an orange twist, hold a whole orange in the palm of your hand and, using a canelle or paring knife, cut into the orange peel, trying to avoid grabbing too much white pith. In a smooth and even motion, roll the orange around in your hand to cut a strip of the peel with the knife as you go. Once you have a long strand of orange peel, wrap it around two fingers and squeeze one section to keep it curled. Place on the edge of the glass with two-thirds of the peel in the cocktail.

CUCUMBER LOONIES

yield: serves 6–8 · prep time: 15 minutes + 30 minutes–3 hours to marinate

Ingredients
5 miniature cucumbers
¼ small white onion, sliced lengthwise
1½ Tbsp rice wine vinegar
2 tsp poppy or black sesame seeds
Sea salt and black pepper

Method
Peel and slice the cucumbers into 1-inch-thick rounds.

In a medium bowl, toss the cucumbers with the onions and vinegar. Refrigerate, uncovered, for at least 30 minutes and up to 3 hours.

Transfer to a serving bowl, sprinkle the poppy seeds overtop, season with salt and pepper, and serve with toothpicks on the side as flatware.

PHYLLO CHEESE ROLLS

yield: serves 6–8 · prep time: 20 minutes + overnight
to thaw · cook time: 15 minutes

Ingredients

1½ cups crumbled feta cheese
⅔ cup cream cheese
2 green onions, thinly sliced
⅔ cup curly parsley, finely chopped
2 tsp thyme leaves
½ tsp black pepper
4 (18- x 14-inch) sheets frozen phyllo, thawed
½ cup olive oil

Method

Preheat the oven to 325°F. Line a baking sheet
with parchment paper.

In a medium mixing bowl, combine both cheeses,
green onions, parsley, thyme, and pepper.
Mix thoroughly then set aside.

Remove the phyllo sheets from the fridge and
dampen some paper towels.

Lay the stacked phyllo sheets on a cutting board in front
of you. Using a sharp knife, cut them into four equal-
sized rectangles (they'll be about 9 x 7 inches each).

You'll be working with 1 piece of phyllo at a time.
Keep the other pieces covered with the damp paper
towels to prevent them from drying out. They need
to be soft and moist so you can roll them.

Brush the piece with oil. Wet your hands, then take
about 2 Tbsp of the cheese mixture and form it into
a log. Place it along the long bottom edge of the
phyllo. Roll the phyllo over the cheese mixture,
tucking in the ends as you go.

Place the phyllo roll on the lined baking sheet, seam
side down, and repeat with the remaining cheese
mixture and phyllo. Cover the finished rolls with
damp paper towels as you work to keep them moist
before cooking. If the phyllo dries out, it can crack
or split when it's baking.

Brush the top of each roll with some oil. Bake until
golden brown, about 15 minutes. Let the rolls rest
for 5 minutes, then cut in half on a bias and serve.

RADISHES WITH BUTTER + FLAVORED SALTS

yield: serves 6–8 · prep time: 20 minutes

Ingredients

HERBES DE PROVENCE SALT BLEND
½ cup kosher salt
1½ tsp herbes de Provence

PINK SALT BLEND
½ cup pink Himalayan salt
1½ tsp sweet paprika

RADISHES
2 bunches French radishes, stems on
1 cup European-style butter, softened (see note)
½ cup Maldon sea salt

Method

FOR THE HERBES DE PROVENCE SALT BLEND
In a small bowl, mix together the salt and herbes de
Provence.

FOR THE PINK SALT BLEND
In a separate small bowl, mix together the salt and
paprika.

FOR THE RADISHES
Wash and trim the radishes, leaving 1 inch of the
stem. Place them in a bowl of ice water and refrigerate until ready to serve.

TO SERVE
Arrange the radishes on a large platter. Place the
butter, Maldon salt, and salt blends in small bowls
and set the bowls on the platter. Guests can dip the
radishes in the butter, then in the salt of their choice.
This is a traditional way to enjoy radishes, and in our
opinion, it's way better than eating them plain!

Note

European butter is typically churned for longer than
North American butter and has a higher fat content,
resulting in a richer, softer texture with a brighter
color. If you can't find European butter, any type
will do.

MUSSELS + SHRIMP WITH PASTA IN ARRABIATA SAUCE

yield: serves 6–8 · prep time: 30 minutes · cook time: 15 minutes

Ingredients

1 lb long pasta (spaghetti or fettuccine would be ideal)

½ cup olive oil, divided

1 yellow onion, finely diced

6 garlic cloves, minced

2 (each 32 oz) jars arrabiata or tomato sauce (see note)

4 lb mussels, pre-washed and debearded (see note)

2 lb pre-cooked shrimp (16/20 count)

1 cup curly parsley, finely chopped

2 tsp chili flakes, optional

Method

Bring a large pot of salted water to a boil over high heat. Cook the pasta according to the package directions. Drain, toss with ¼ cup of the oil, and set aside while you prepare the sauce.

In a large pan with a tight-fitting lid, heat the remaining ¼ cup of oil over medium heat. Add the onions and garlic and cook, stirring occasionally, until translucent, about 5 minutes.

Add the sauce and increase the heat to high to bring the sauce to a simmer, stirring occasionally. Once it's simmering, add the mussels and shrimp and stir to ensure that they're coated in the sauce.

Cover with the lid and cook until all the mussels have opened, about 5 minutes. Discard any that haven't opened.

Divide the pasta among individual bowls and top with the mussels and shrimp sauce. Sprinkle some parsley and chili flakes (if using) overtop before serving.

Notes

- If you can't find arrabiata sauce at the grocery store, add 1 Tbsp of dried chili flakes to a 32 oz jar of tomato or marinara sauce.
- Before you add the mussels to the pot, look for any that aren't completely closed and gently tap them with a spoon to make sure they aren't bad. The mussels should slowly close when tapped, but if they don't shut completely, they are not good to eat and should be discarded.
- Although we prefer to serve the mussels, shrimp, and pasta in the same bowl, we recommend plating the seafood and pasta separately on your table in case some guests prefer not to mix it all together. Small gestures like this, thinking ahead to what your guests may or make not like, will make your guests feel welcomed.

SIMPLE GREEN SALAD

yield: serves 6–8 · prep time: 15 minutes

Ingredients

8 cups leafy greens (Bibb, frisée,
    or red oak are ideal)

2 shallots, peeled and thinly sliced

½ cup olive oil

3 Tbsp lemon juice

1 tsp grainy Dijon mustard

Sea salt and black pepper

Method

Place the greens and sliced shallots in a salad bowl.

In a small bowl or mason jar, whisk together the oil, lemon juice, Dijon, salt, and pepper. Drizzle this vinaigrette over the greens, toss well, and serve immediately.

Note

You can prepare the dressing and clean your greens ahead of time, but try not to combine them until a few seconds before you bring your salad to the table.

SEB SAYS

If you want to prepare the salad a bit early, try leaving the lettuce wrapped in a damp paper towel in the fridge. This will keep it fresh, crisp, and ready to toss with the dressing right before you bring it to the table.

LEMON TIRAMISU

yield: serves 6–8 · prep time: 30 minutes + 2 hours to chill

Ingredients

LEMON SIMPLE SYRUP
2 cups granulated sugar
1 lemon, grated zest and juice of

TIRAMISU
2 cups whipping (36%) cream
3 Tbsp granulated sugar
24–32 ladyfinger cookies
1½ cups lemon simple syrup
1 cup store-bought lemon curd
1½ cups mascarpone, softened
2 pints raspberries
10 mint leaves

Method

FOR THE SIMPLE SYRUP
Place the sugar, lemon zest and juice, and 2 cups of water in a saucepan set over medium heat. Bring to a simmer and stir to dissolve all the sugar. Remove from the heat, let cool to room temperature, and refrigerate in the saucepan until ready to use.

FOR THE TIRAMISU
Set aside 6 to 8 rocks glasses or other short glasses for serving. We're flexible with the size of glass you use for this—worst case, you've got one left over.

Using a stand mixer or handheld mixer, beat the cream and sugar on high speed until fluffy and stiff peaks form, about 8 minutes.

Dip 2 ladyfinger cookies in the simple syrup and place them in the bottom of a glass, breaking them in half if required.

Layer 3 Tbsp of lemon curd, followed by 2 Tbsp mascarpone, and then 3 Tbsp of whipped cream on top of the ladyfinger cookies. Dip 2 more ladyfingers in the syrup and place overtop. Repeat with the remaining glasses.

Garnish each glass with raspberries and mint. Refrigerate for 2 hours or ideally overnight before serving, and serve chilled.

Notes
- If you can't find lemon curd at your grocery store, you can use instant lemon or vanilla pudding.
- You can use 2 cups of lemon liqueur instead of the simple syrup if you prefer.

While most of our entertaining concepts now revolve around entertaining adults, we remember when our children were younger and hosting friends with their kids was a big part of our life. We have never been afraid to entertain with our boys, and we always enjoyed finding playful ways to include them and their friends in the entertaining process from a young age. Although the main focus of a playdate is the kids, there's no reason the adults can't have fun as well.

Nowadays, parents are making more of an effort than ever before to build healthy eating habits for their children. And while I am 100% on board with this, trying to sneak vegetables into cupcakes or swapping out ground beef for ground cauliflower in a burger just isn't going to work. Instead, look at how you can take foods that kids already love and add a healthier twist by tweaking recipes and making minor adjustments to your ingredient choices. All the recipes in this chapter are made with fresh, healthy ingredients that any kid would love. And when it comes to kids getting their daily dose of veggies . . . well, keep reading!

As the saying goes, kids will be kids, which is why entertaining a younger audience is all about letting go of perfection and simply going with the flow. Having raised two boys ourselves, we know this is easier said than done, but many of our fondest memories include a backyard or kitchen full of kids. It may have been absolute mayhem for a couple of hours, but it was nothing that a few glasses (or bottles) of wine couldn't fix! We have passed on our love of entertaining to our boys, who now find themselves hosting their friends more often than most young adults.

The menu and drink options on the following pages are perfect for hosting an after-school playdate, Sunday afternoon get-together, or anything in between!

FUN WITH KIDS

TIP *A self-serve menu helps relieve some of the pressure of hosting while also showing your guests how easy hosting with kids can be. Once your guests see that it's not as difficult as they thought, we have no doubt they will happily reciprocate in the near future.*

SHEILA SAYS *Set expectations early regarding behavior and manners. No parent or kid will like the surprise of arriving at your home and being told the rules and most kids LOVE to perform in front of an audience! I suggest that parents make a big deal of telling their kids that they are invited to an exclusive party. This builds some excitement, makes them feel that they are a part of something special, and makes them more likely to behave well on the day.*

SETTING

Since the focus of this chapter is entertaining with kids, we'll be setting the table for kids and kids only. The adults can mingle and enjoy some cocktails and appetizers while still keeping an eye on the young ones.

Planning a menu of easy-to-eat finger foods eliminates the need for an elaborate place setting with multiple sets of plates and cutlery. We recommend classic white plateware, since the rest of the table will be so colorful, and minimal flatware. Flatware isn't necessary for finger foods, but if you want to add a fork to each place setting just in case, that's totally fine. Keep in mind that there will likely be a few topples and spills during the meal, which is why we also recommend using plastic cups. Whimsical straws (ideally, resuable ones) and an assortment of accents keep the table attractive to a younger audience. Leave space to put down the sharing platters—when it comes to meals with kids, we like to serve everything family-style.

As for fresh florals, we incorporate them into all our get-togethers, and entertaining with kids is no exception. Look for simple, bright floral stems and present them in several small, low vases like milk bottles or mason jars to prevent them from being knocked over by the kids' busy hands.

We all know kids can get restless while sitting at the table, so it's important to have lots of activities to keep them busy. An easy and fun trick that also simplifies your cleanup is to set the table with craft paper instead of a tablecloth. Not only will this help you prepare for the inevitable spills, but it also serves as a drawing surface if you supply some crayons. The kids can scribble to their heart's content before or while they eat!

In addition to the craft tablecloth, make your party memorable by providing the kids with a keepsake that they can decorate and take home. We suggest a mason jar filled with crayons, age-appropriate small crafts and toys, and a coloring book, notebook, or bedroom doorknob sign that they can personalize. This is also the perfect opportunity to get your own little one involved in entertaining by helping you with shopping for things to put in the jars for their guests and then helping to fill them.

TIP

Serve all the dishes on a variety of simple, inexpensive platters to help make your cleanup easier. Even consider some disposable elements (recyclable, of course)!

WHAT'S ON THE MENU

Our menu for a kids' meal is designed for children under the age of 10 and focuses entirely on informal dishes that can be eaten in any order, so there's no need for traditional appetizers and entrées. You can bring everything to the table at once or in waves and let the kids treat it like a buffet.

COURSES

The first item that we like to include at a kids' dinner party is a Crudités Pepper Cup: a cup of cut-up veggies. While normally we would use a small glass or bowl as a cup for veggie sticks, for this menu we recommend slicing off the top of a bell pepper and hollowing it out. (And yes, one of the ingredients in this recipe is actually slightly cooked!) Showing your kids that food can be fun and inventive is a great way of getting them excited to eat their veggies, not to mention saving you a round of dishes!

Next, we like to serve what seems like a fan-favorite among kids of all ages and palates: homemade chicken fingers! Serve them in steel pails with plum dip or ketchup on the side and even the pickiest of eaters will brighten up when they see these coming to the table. You can make your own homemade chicken fingers from our recipe, but if you want to save time, there are also some great healthy store-bought chicken fingers that work just as well.

Sticking with the theme of fan-favorites, homemade pizza pockets are a fun DIY project that your kids can help you make. The simplest version of this recipe requires only pizza dough, sauce, and shredded cheese, but it can accommodate toppings too. A major benefit of this dish is that the pizza pockets can be frozen for up to 3 months, making an impromptu play date that much easier.

Peanut Butter + Jelly Fruit Lollipops and fun-shaped Grilled Cheese Cut-Outs are two more easy ways to brighten up the menu. Both dishes are contemporary takes on traditional recipes that are sure to have every child excited about dinner time. Check to make sure there are no peanut allergies before preparing the lollipops. (See below for some easy ways to accommodate common allergies.)

Few children will have the appetite to eat every course listed above, so you can include or omit certain dishes based on what your kids like and how many kids you're hosting. If you make a bit extra, don't worry, as adults tend to steal the odd grilled cheese or chicken finger when nobody's looking.

For the adults, we like to serve two easy-to-make appetizers that they can graze on while socializing or looking over their little ones. The first dish is Pull-Apart Cheesy Garlic Bread. The second, a basic Charcuterie + Cheese Board, is the perfect complement to the bread. See pages 14–15 for instructions on how to build the perfectly balanced charcuterie board.

Finally, for dessert we are serving a Watermelon "Pizza"! It's a great and tasty way to incorporate yogurt and fruit into your kids' menu or even the adults' menu too.

WHAT'S ON THE BAR

The idea for the drinks section of this party is to have two kid-friendly options that can also work for the adults. For this reason, we suggest putting out carafes of fresh juice with matching frozen garnishes—typically, we offer pink grapefruit, pineapple, and cranberry juices but use whatever your guests are likely to enjoy. We also like to put out flavored sparkling water. Any sparkling water works, but we recommend sugar-free options like La Croix, San Pellegrino Essenza, or bubly. Put the bottles in an ice bucket on the bar about 30 minutes before you expect your guests so they're chilled and ready to drink.

Have a few different types of alcohols or wine available to mix with the kids' drinks to create a cocktail. Vodka, prosecco, and white wine all mix exceptionally well with the non-alcoholic beverages mentioned above. Keep the alcoholic add-ons in an ice bucket so they stay chilled throughout the party.

FUN WITH KIDS

COCKTAILS

KID'S COCKTAIL (P71)

ADULT'S COCKTAIL (P71)

KIDS MENU

CRUDITÉS PEPPER CUPS (P73)

HOMEMADE CHICKEN FINGERS (P73)

PIZZA POCKETS (P74)

PEANUT BUTTER + JELLY FRUIT

LOLLIPOPS (P77)

GRILLED CHEESE CUT-OUTS (P77)

ADULT MENU

PULL-APART CHEESY GARLIC
BREAD (P79)

CHARCUTERIE + CHEESE BOARD (P79)

DESSERT

WATERMELON "PIZZA" (P80)

PARTY COUNTDOWN:

FUN WITH KIDS

3 THREE DAYS BEFORE

- ○ Send a reminder email or text to your guests with details about the party.

- ○ Make your grocery and alcohol list.

- ○ Check you have enough plates and glasses for your guests.

- ○ Shop for reusable straws, craft paper for the tablecloth, and craft supplies to fill the mason jars.

- ○ Grocery shop, including for sparkling water and juice, and stock up on alcohol.

2 TWO DAYS BEFORE

- ○ Make and freeze the pizza pockets.

- ○ Have your children help fill the mason jars for the crafts.

TIME– SAVING TIP

Use store-bought ingredients. Frozen pizza dough, shredded cheese, pre-cut veggies, and frozen chicken fingers can help turn recipes into assembly only!

1 THE DAY BEFORE

- ☐ Freeze the fruit for the garnishes.
- ☐ Cut vegetables for crudités and store them in an airtight container in the fridge.
- ☐ Buy flowers, trim them, and store them in water overnight.

0 THE DAY OF

- ☐ Prepare the floral arrangements and set the table.
- ☐ Finish assembling the vegetable cups.
- ☐ Prepare the chicken fingers.
- ☐ Bake the pizza pockets.
- ☐ Assemble the peanut butter + jelly fruit lollipops.
- ☐ Prepare the grilled cheese cut-outs.
- ☐ Prepare the watermelon "pizza."
- ☐ Prepare the charcuterie board.

I like to prepare little bowls of frozen garnishes to match the juices as a fun way to give a drink extra flavor and keep it cold once poured. Keep the bowls of garnish in the freezer until your guests arrive so they remain super cold and don't dry out.

KID'S COCKTAIL

yield: makes 1 cocktail · prep time: 2 minutes

Ingredients

¾ cup pink grapefruit, pineapple, or cranberry juice
¼ cup soda water

Method

Combine the juice and soda water in a kid-friendly
cup and serve!

ADULT'S COCKTAIL

yield: makes 1 cocktail · prep time: 2 minutes

Ingredients

¾ cup pink grapefruit, pineapple, or cranberry juice
1 oz vodka
¼ cup soda water

Method

Combine the juice and vodka in a short rocks glass.
Top with soda water and serve.

CRUDITÉS PEPPER
CUPS

HOMEMADE
CHICKEN
FINGERS

CRUDITÉS PEPPER CUPS

yield: serves 6 · prep time: 30 minutes · cook time: 3 minutes

Ingredients

6 field carrots
6 celery ribs
6 large bell peppers, any color
1½ tsp sea salt
12 green beans
1¼ cups hummus, ranch dressing, or other vegetable dip
15 mini cucumbers, halved lengthwise
1 pint mixed cherry tomatoes

Method

Cut the carrots and celery sticks into quarters about 3- to 5-inches long, and set aside. You'll have 24 sticks each.

Cut a thin slice of stem and top off each bell pepper, just enough to make them stand up straight but not so much that you puncture the bottom. You don't want the hummus to spill through. Remove the seeds and membrane.

Place the salt and 4 cups of water in a pot over high heat and bring to a boil. Prepare an ice bath.

Once the water is boiling, add the beans and boil for 3 minutes. Transfer to the ice bath immediately to stop the cooking process.

Fill each pepper cup with about 3 Tbsp of hummus.

Insert 4 carrot sticks, 4 celery sticks, 2 beans, 5 cucumber halves, and a few cherry tomatoes into the hummus in each cup. Serve immediately.

HOMEMADE CHICKEN FINGERS

yield: serves 6–8 · prep time: 25 minutes · cook time: 30 minutes

Ingredients

4 boneless, skinless chicken breasts
1 cup plain breadcrumbs
1½ tsp kosher salt
1 tsp black pepper
1 tsp sweet paprika
2 large eggs
Plum sauce and/or ketchup, for serving

Method

Preheat the oven to 375°F. Line a large baking sheet with parchment paper. Place a wire rack on top of the baking sheet and coat it with cooking spray.

Cut each chicken breast into finger-sized strips. You should get 4 or 5 strips from each breast.

In a shallow dish, combine the breadcrumbs, salt, pepper, and paprika.

In a second shallow dish, whisk the eggs. Set the eggs beside the breadcrumbs. Working with 1 strip at a time, dip the chicken into the eggs and then toss in the breadcrumbs. Pat gently to ensure the breadcrumbs adhere to the chicken, then place on the wire rack.

Once all the chicken has been breaded and placed on the wire rack, spray the top of the chicken with cooking spray. Bake with the sprayed side down for 15 minutes, then flip over each strip, and bake until golden brown, 10–15 minutes, ensuring that the internal temperature is 165°F.

Remove the chicken fingers from the oven and season to taste with salt and pepper. Serve warm with plum sauce or ketchup—or both!—on the side.

PIZZA POCKETS

yield: serves 6–8 · prep time: 30 minutes + 45 minutes to rest · cook time: 25 minutes

Ingredients

1½ lb prepared pizza dough

¼ cup all-purpose flour

½ cup pizza sauce + more for serving

8 slices pepperoni

2 cups shredded mozzarella (about 1 ball)

¾ cup sliced white mushrooms

½ green bell pepper, julienned

Method

Remove the dough from the refrigerator and let it sit at room temperature for 45 minutes. Preheat the oven to 425°F. Line a baking sheet with parchment paper and dust with flour.

Cut the dough into 8 equal-sized pieces. Roll each piece into a ball, and then use your hands or a rolling pin to shape it into a 4- to 5-inch round. Place the rounds on the prepared baking sheet. You may need to bake the pockets in batches.

Place 1 Tbsp of sauce, 2 pepperoni slices, and 1½ Tbsp of mozzarella (in that order) in the center of 4 of the dough rounds. Be careful not to overfill them. Place 1 Tbsp of sauce, 2 mushroom slices, a few slices of green pepper, and 1½ Tbsp of mozzarella (in that order) in the center of the other 4 rounds.

Next, brush the edge of each dough round with water and carefully fold the dough over itself to form a half-moon shape. Firmly push down the edges with your fingers or a fork dipped in flour to seal the pockets shut. Dust the top of each pizza pocket with flour.

Bake until the pizza pocket tops are golden and the dough is cooked through, 25 minutes. Serve immediately with extra pizza sauce on the side.

Note

If you're making these in advance, freeze the pizza pockets on a baking tray for about 1 hour then transfer to a freezer-safe airtight container and freeze for up to 3 months. Bake from frozen in a 375°F oven until golden brown, 30–45 minutes.

PEANUT BUTTER +
JELLY FRUIT
LOLLIPOPS

GRILLED CHEESE
CUT-OUTS

PEANUT BUTTER + JELLY FRUIT LOLLIPOPS

yield: serves 6–8 · prep time: 20 minutes + 1 hour to chill

Ingredients
2 cups strawberry jam
1½ cups smooth peanut butter
6 slices soft white or whole wheat sandwich bread
12–16 (10-inch-long) bamboo skewers
1 pint large blueberries
1 pint blackberries
½ quart strawberries, stems removed
1 cup red and green grapes
Dry rice, for serving

Method
In a large mixing bowl, mix together the jam and peanut butter until well combined.

Cut the crusts off each slice of bread. Using a rolling pin, roll each slice of bread to ¼-inch thick.

Spread the jam and peanut butter mixture on each slice of bread in an even layer. Roll the slice of bread into a tight log. Wrap in plastic wrap and refrigerate for 1 hour.

Remove the plastic wrap and cut each log into 4 pinwheels, each about 1-inch thick.

Gently insert a skewer lengthwise through a pinwheel, then place a blueberry, blackberry, strawberry, or grape on the skewer. Continue to add pinwheels and fruit, alternating types, but be sure to leave 1–2 inches of room at the end of the skewer. Repeat with the remaining skewers.

When you're ready to serve, place some dry rice in a glass vase. Place the skewers in the vase, with the empty ends down, so that the rice doesn't stick to the lollipops.

GRILLED CHEESE CUT-OUTS

yield: serves 6–8 · prep time: 20 minutes + 1 hour to chill · cook time: 30–40 minutes

Ingredients
12 slices soft white bread
½ cup butter, softened
12 American cheese slices
Ketchup, for dipping

Method
Preheat a large nonstick skillet over medium-high heat.

Butter 1 side of a slice of bread and place 2 slices of cheese on the unbuttered side. Place the bread in the skillet, buttered side down. Spread butter on a second slice of bread, and close the sandwich buttered side up. You'll likely be able to fit 2 sandwiches in the pan, but be careful not to overcrowd it.

Cook each sandwich, flipping once, until golden brown on both sides and the cheese has melted slightly, about 4 minutes per side. Repeat to make 6 full sandwiches.

Allow the sandwiches to cool completely. Refrigerate covered for 1 hour, with pieces of parchment paper separating the sandwiches if you are stacking them.

Using a cookie cutter or sharp knife, cut each sandwich into a variety of shapes. The sandwiches will stay together better once they're cold.

To serve, reheat the cut sandwiches in a 200°F oven for 10 minutes or simply let them come to room temperature. Don't forget the ketchup for dipping.

PULL-APART CHEESY GARLIC BREAD

yield: serves 6–8 · prep time: 10 minutes · cook time: 15 minutes

Ingredients

1 large white baguette
5 oz Boursin Garlic + Fine Herbs cheese
5 slices aged cheddar cheese
5 slices mozzarella or provolone cheese
½ cup store-bought garlic and herb butter
3 Tbsp flat-leaf parsley leaves
Grated parmigiano-reggiano cheese, for serving
Tomato sauce or Caesar salad dressing, for dipping

Method

Preheat the oven to 375°F. Line a baking sheet with parchment paper.

Without cutting all the way through, cut the baguette in slices ¼- to ½-inch thick. You should have 10 cuts in the bread.

Spread the Boursin liberally between each cut. Insert half a slice each of cheddar and mozzarella into the cuts. Spread the garlic butter over the top of the baguette.

Place the baguette on the prepared baking sheet and bake until the cheese is melted and the bread is golden, about 15 minutes.

Garnish with the parsley and parmigiano-reggiano, and serve immediately with tomato sauce or Caesar dressing on the side for dipping.

Note

The baguette can be kept in the oven on the "Keep Warm" setting (usually 150°F) for up to 2 hours.

CHARCUTERIE + CHEESE BOARD

yield: serves 6–8 · prep time: 25 minutes + 1 hour to rest

Ingredients

MEAT + CHEESE
3½ oz blue cheese
3½ oz washed rind cheese, such as camembert or brie
3½ oz hard sharp cheese, such as parmigiano-reggiano
3½ oz chèvre
2 oz spicy soppressata
2 oz Genoa salami
2 oz prosciutto
2 oz coppa

ACCOMPANIMENTS
Dates
Marcona almonds
Fresh figs
Cornichons
Mini pickled peppers
Honeycomb
Kettle chips, various flavors

Method

Arrange all the ingredients on a cutting board—see our tips on pages 14–15. Allow to sit at room temperature for at least 1 hour before serving so all the cheeses and meats are at their most flavorful.

WATERMELON "PIZZA"

yield: serves 6 · prep time: 10 minutes

Ingredients

1 small watermelon

½ cup vanilla Greek yogurt

6 gooseberries, leaves removed

6 large blueberries

6 blackberries

3 Tbsp pomegranate seeds

Method

Cut the watermelon at the center (or through the thickest part) into a 2-inch-thick disk (you can cut up the remaining watermelon in small chunks to serve on the side or save it for a later use).

Place the watermelon disk onto a cutting board and cut across it to make 6 slices. Spread the yogurt onto each slice and top with gooseberries, blueberries, blackberries, and pomegranate seeds. Serve immediately.

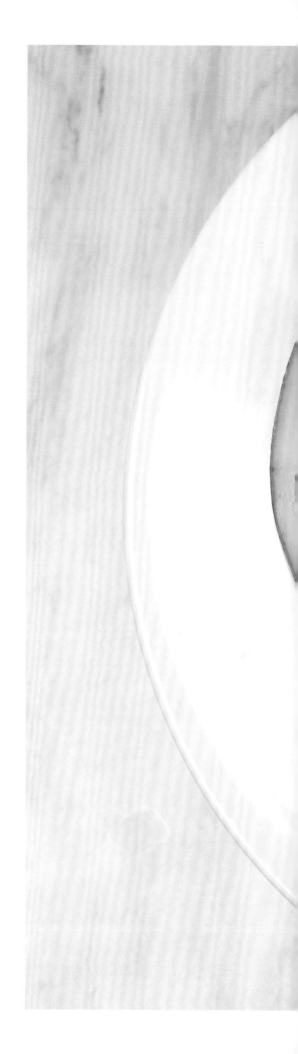

1

SIMPLE ENTER- TAINING

SHEILA SAYS
I like to serve Aperol spritzes in large fishbowl-like wine glasses that I call "piscine" glasses since it feels like you're being served a full swimming pool in a single glass!

As the temperature rises and daylight extends into the early hours of the evening, we love to take advantage of the beautiful weather by entertaining outdoors.

"Al fresco" is an Italian term that translates literally as "in the open." We use the term for all of our outdoor entertaining to add a touch of elegance to an otherwise casual evening. Coupled with a simple but delicious menu and chic cocktails, a simply set table with a few added comforts is often all that is needed to transport your guests to the Mediterranean.

One of our favorite things about outdoor dining is that it can offer a break from the distractions of technology, provided your guests are on board. Al fresco dinners are often quite intimate evenings with small groups of people. As hard as it may be, we encourage our guests to disconnect from their electronics and enjoy each other's company phone-free. When you're dining outdoors it's important to create a friendly and relaxed ambience that will set the tone for the entire evening and create the perfect space to have uninterrupted conversations.

By now you've probably realized that the key to this meal is simplicity. If you use our menu and cocktail recommendations on the following pages, we have no doubt that you'll be ready to host your own al fresco dinner parties all summer long.

EASY AL FRESCO DINNER

SEB SAYS *Sheila and I like to make sure one of us is always with our guests. As Sheila leads our guests to the table, I try to sneak into the kitchen to plate the first course. We swap positions throughout the dinner so one of us always remains at the table with our guests.*

SETTING

Since we're focusing on simplicity, we recommend starting with a crisp white tablecloth to set the tone as light, bright, and airy. Next, we add some accents of color.

When we imagine the colors of coastal dining in southern Italy, the first thing that pops into our heads is soft pastels: blues, greens, and pale purples. Instead of using regular white plateware, try incorporating dishes with pastel hues to highlight the relaxed Mediterranean vibe you're trying to channel. Pastel accents are especially great when your menu is filled with bright colors as they provide a nice background without competing with the deep tones of the dishes.

If you have extra time, a fun DIY activity for your al fresco dinner is to make paper bag napkin rings. Simply cut a paper bag into clean strips, slide each one over a napkin, and then add your cutlery. Though traditional napkin rings work just as well, we try to incorporate homemade ones whenever possible to add a personal touch.

For florals in this setting, we like to keep it simple, of course, and use a long garland runner as the main centerpiece for our table. Not only does this add to the intimate feeling of an al fresco dinner with an outdoor garden touch, but it also helps connect your table to the greenery in your backyard. Well-placed small, clear votive candles are a great option if you're looking to add easy ambient lighting as the sun goes down.

Finally, give some thought to providing a little added comfort. If you've visited cafés in Europe during the shoulder seasons you may have noticed the small pillows or throws on the back of each chair. The idea is simultaneously chic and cozy, especially when the evenings cool down. If you choose to do this for your al fresco dinner party—and it's not essential for every al fresco event—make sure that your pillows and throws match the color scheme of the rest of the table. We like to offer white, machine-washable throw blankets—they always get used, and it makes our lives so much easier to be able to wash them afterwards.

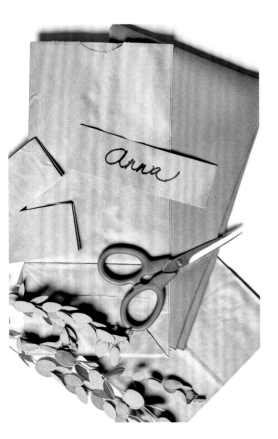

Anna

TIP

If you're looking to be more environmentally responsible (which we always strive for when we entertain), try reusing wine or alcohol bottles as carafes for water by washing them and removing the labels.

WHAT'S ON THE MENU

We begin our al fresco dining experience by letting our guests pick at a few quick and easy welcome snacks: Marinated Olives + Chips and slices of warm Tomato Focaccia. While the focaccia and chips can be prepared a few minutes before guests arrive, we recommend preparing the olives the day before and letting them marinate overnight to deepen their flavor.

COURSES

As you and your guests transition from your cocktails to the table, we suggest plating the first course of tonight's meal, a bright and fresh gazpacho. Since it's served cold, the gazpacho can be prepared the night before your al fresco dinner, so it won't pull you away from the table for more than a few minutes.

What would your coastal al fresco dinner be without a pasta dish! Sheila's Fusilli with Prosciutto + Cherry Tomatoes is the perfect recipe for this occasion as it adds to the intimate atmosphere with its simple and colorful presentation. This is one of our go-to dishes because it can be served either at room temperature (a pasta salad of sorts) or warmed. Both options are great for outdoor summer entertaining.

Our third course of the evening is Seared Beef Steak—tagliata di manzo in Italian—coupled with a zesty Arugula Salad. Unlike the first two courses, this one requires a bit of time in the kitchen. Once the meat has cooked and rested, though, this dish is an easy sharing course around the table.

Finally, we can't imagine a better way to close out your al fresco dinner than by offering a classic Italian dessert: Affogato. If you don't know what that is, it's simply a shot of espresso, or an espresso substitute, poured over vanilla ice cream and garnished with crushed amaretti cookies. While you can pour the coffee over the ice cream before serving it, we like to bring the two ingredients to the table separately so guests can pour their own coffee for the added wow factor.

WHAT'S ON THE BAR

Since most al fresco dining is done in small, intimate groups, we try not to overwhelm our guests with too many cocktail options. For this meal we'll be offering two signature cocktails that pair well with any summer backyard get-together.

To continue with our Mediterranean theme, the two cocktails we'll be serving both feature Italian bitter liqueurs. The Aperol Spritz uses prosecco for a slightly sweeter taste and the Campari + Soda is crisp and tart, making them both ideal for a summer evening. These timeless summer cocktails are easy to mix and will appeal to a wide variety of guests. Their colors complement each other, so we like to serve a few of each on a tray, letting our guests pick their favorite or even try both. We like to use a tall wine glass for the Aperol Spritz and a short rocks glass for the Campari + Soda.

Though we prefer sticking to cocktails for the duration of this dinner, it's never a bad idea to have a bottle or two of wine chilling nearby. A light, crispy pinot grigio tends to do the trick and will pair beautifully with each course.

EASY AL FRESCO DINNER

COCKTAILS

APEROL SPRITZ (P92)

CAMPARI + SODA (P92)

SNACKS

MARINATED OLIVES + CHIPS (P93)

TOMATO FOCACCIA (P93)

FIRST COURSE

GAZPACHO (P95)

SECOND COURSE

SHEILA'S FUSILLI WITH PROSCIUTTO +
CHERRY TOMATOES (P95)

THIRD COURSE

SEARED BEEF STEAK WITH
ARUGULA SALAD (P96)

DESSERT

AFFOGATO (P98)

PARTY COUNTDOWN:

EASY AL FRESCO DINNER

3 THREE DAYS BEFORE

- ○ Send a reminder email or text to your guests with details about the evening.

- ○ Make a grocery and alcohol list.

- ○ Make sure you have enough plates and glasses for your guests.

- ○ Grocery shop (but leave the beef until the day of the dinner) and stock up at the liquor store.

- ○ Let the tomatoes for the gazpacho ripen in a sunny spot or next to other fruits.

2 TWO DAYS BEFORE

- ○ Make the napkin rings.

- ○ Check the weather forecast for the day of your dinner and prepare accordingly. Collect throw blankets, bug spray, sun umbrellas, etc. to make sure your guests are comfortable al fresco.

TIME-SAVING TIPS

Use frozen focaccia and bake according to the package directions.

Boil the water for the pasta before your guests arrive. Once it's boiling, turn it off and cover with a lid. When you're ready to cook your pasta, turn the heat back on and the pasta water will boil faster since your water is already halfway there.

1 THE DAY BEFORE

- ◯ Buy flowers, trim them, and store them in water overnight. Or look around your garden to see what you can use from there.

- ◯ Prepare the marinated olives and refrigerate in an airtight container.

- ◯ Prepare the gazpacho and refrigerate in an airtight container.

- ◯ Prepare the garlic and tomatoes for the pasta and refrigerate in an airtight container.

0 THE DAY OF

- ◯ Prepare the floral ararngements and set the table.

- ◯ Buy beef.

- ◯ Buy freshly baked focaccia.

- ◯ Chill the wine.

- ◯ Chill the serving vessels for the affogatos.

While many people might assume that using an oven is the best way to warm up focaccia, we recommend warming it up on the barbecue! This allows a nice crust to form on the outside of the focaccia while also giving it beautiful grill marks.

LEFT

CLOCKWISE: APEROL SPRITZ, CHIPS, MARINATED OLIVES, CAMPARI + SODA

ABOVE

CLOCKWISE: CHIPS, TOMATO FOCACCIA, WHITE FOCACCIA, MARINATED OLIVES

COCKTAILS + SNACKS

APEROL SPRITZ

yield: makes 1 cocktail · prep time: 5 minutes

Ingredients
2 oz prosecco
1¼ oz aperol
Soda water
1 orange slice

Method
In a tall wine glass filled with ice, gently stir together the prosecco and aperol. Top with a splash of soda water and garnish with the orange.

CAMPARI + SODA

yield: makes 1 cocktail · prep time: 5 minutes

Ingredients
2 oz Campari
Soda water
1 orange slice

Method
Add the Campari to a short rocks glass filled with ice. Fill to the top with soda water and garnish with the orange.

MARINATED OLIVES + CHIPS

yield: serves 6–8 · prep time: 20 minutes + 1 hour to marinate · cook time: 2 minutes

Ingredients

2 lemons
2 oranges
1 cup + 2½ Tbsp olive oil
4 thyme sprigs, leaves removed and chopped
2 rosemary sprigs, leaves removed and chopped
2 oregano sprigs, leaves removed and chopped
1 Tbsp black pepper
1 tsp sea salt
1½ Tbsp coriander seeds
1⅔ cups Kalamata olives
1⅔ cups green queen olives
4–6 cups kettle chips, any flavor

Method

Using a vegetable peeler or paring knife, peel long thick strips of lemon and orange zest. Set aside, then juice the lemons and oranges.

In a large bowl, combine the lemon and orange juices and zest, oil, thyme, rosemary, oregano, pepper, and salt. Whisk well.

Preheat a large skillet over low heat, then add the coriander seeds. Toast until light golden brown, 1–2 minutes. Using a mortar and pestle, crush the seeds slightly (or place them on a clean dish cloth and use the pan for this task). Add the crushed seeds to the dressing.

Place the olives in a shallow baking tray, just large enough to hold them snugly without crowding, pour the dressing overtop, and marinate at room temperature for at least 1 hour. Transfer to a few small bowls to serve, with the chips in separate bowls on the side.

TOMATO FOCACCIA

yield: serves 6–8 · prep time: 10 minutes · cook time: 10 minutes

Ingredients

1 (8- to 10-inch) store-bought, pre-baked focaccia or flat bread
1 Tbsp olive oil
4–5 sundried tomatoes, cut into thick strips (see note)
2 oregano sprigs, leaves removed and chopped
1 thyme sprig, leaves removed and chopped
1 rosemary sprig, leaves removed and chopped
2 Tbsp grated parmigiano-reggiano
¼ tsp chili flakes, optional

Method

Preheat the barbecue over medium-high heat or the oven to 350°F. If you're using the oven, line a baking sheet with parchment paper.

Drizzle the focaccia with the oil. Arrange the sundried tomatoes on the focaccia in an even layer, then sprinkle the oregano, thyme, rosemary, parmigiano-reggiano, and chili flakes (if using) overtop. Warm on the barbecue or in the oven for 5–10 minutes. Cut into strips and serve immediately.

Note

For a white focaccia, omit the sundried tomato.

GAZPACHO

SHEILA'S FUSILLI
WITH PROSCIUTTO +
CHERRY TOMATOES

GAZPACHO

yield: serves 6–8 · prep time: 20 minutes + 1 hour–overnight to chill

Ingredients

2 lb ripe on-the-vine tomatoes or beefsteak tomatoes (about 8–10; see note)

3 garlic cloves

3 pepperoncino rings (1 whole pepperoncino)

2 red bell peppers, roughly chopped

1 English cucumber, peeled, seeds and pulp removed

½ Spanish onion, roughly chopped

½ cup olive oil

3 Tbsp red wine vinegar

1½ tsp honey

1 Tbsp sea salt

½ Tbsp black pepper

6 tsp mascarpone cheese

Method

Put all the ingredients except the mascarpone in a blender or food processor, and blend on high speed until completely smooth. Depending on the size of your blender, you may need to do this in batches. Let the gazpacho sit in the refrigerator for at least 1 hour, or up to overnight. Taste and season with more salt, pepper, or honey if necessary. To serve, ladle the soup into individual bowls, and top each one with 1 tsp of mascarpone.

Note

Gazpacho works best with the ripest summer tomatoes. Purchase your tomatoes a few days in advance and let them ripen on the counter. Place them stem side down on a sunny windowsill or next to other fruits like bananas or apples.

SHEILA'S FUSILLI WITH PROSCIUTTO + CHERRY TOMATOES

yield: serves 6–8 · prep time: 30 minutes + 2 hours–overnight to marinate · cook time: 12 minutes

Ingredients

3 pints cherry tomatoes, halved

1 Tbsp minced garlic

2 lb fusilli

¼ cup olive oil

Sea salt and black pepper

10½ oz prosciutto, sliced paper thin

½ cup basil leaves

6 oz parmigiano-reggiano

Chili flakes, for garnish, optional

Method

In a small bowl, mix the tomatoes with the garlic. Refrigerate for at least 2 hours, or preferably overnight.

In a large pot, cook the pasta in generously salted water according to the package directions until al dente.

Drain the pasta, transfer to a large bowl, add the oil, and toss to coat completely. Season to taste with salt and pepper.

Divide the pasta among six to eight bowls. Arrange the tomatoes, prosciutto, and basil overtop. Using a sharp knife or vegetable peeler, shave some parmigiano-reggiano over everything. Sprinkle with chili flakes (if using) and serve immediately.

SEARED BEEF STEAK WITH ARUGULA SALAD

yield: serves 6–8 · prep time: 20 minutes + 1 hour 10 minutes to rest · cook time: 4–6 minutes

Ingredients

BEEF
1 (2–3 lb) beef tenderloin
2 Tbsp olive oil
2 Tbsp kosher salt
2 Tbsp black pepper

SALAD
5 cups arugula
2 Tbsp lemon juice
1 Tbsp olive oil
½ tsp kosher salt
½ tsp black pepper
2 lemons, cut into rounds, then
    quartered
6 Tbsp grated parmigiano-reggiano

Method

FOR THE BEEF
Remove the beef from the fridge, pat dry, and let sit at room temperature for 1 hour.

Rub all sides of the beef with the oil and season with the salt and pepper.

Heat a large cast iron skillet over high heat. When it's very hot, add the meat and cook for 2 minutes, undisturbed. Flip and cook for another 2 minutes, undisturbed, so you get a good crust and medium-rare inside. Adjust the time and add 1 more minute to each side if you want the meat medium instead of medium-rare.

Transfer to a wire rack and let rest for at least 10 minutes so the juices redistribute. The meat only needs to be warm or room temperature when you serve it. Transfer to a cutting board and cut into thin slices.

FOR THE SALAD
In a medium bowl, toss the arugula with the lemon juice, oil, salt, and pepper.

In the center of a large round platter, pile up the arugula. Arrange the beef slices around the salad. Garnish with the lemons and parmigiano-reggiano.

AFFOGATO

yield: serves 6 · prep time: 10 minutes + 1 hour to chill

Ingredients
1 pint vanilla ice cream
**1 cup + 2 Tbsp espresso or
   strongly brewed coffee**
12 amaretti cookies, crushed

Method
Chill six espresso cups or small glasses in the fridge for
1 hour.

Place 1 scoop of vanilla ice cream in each glass and
immediately pour over 1 shot of espresso or 2–3 Tbsp
strongly brewed coffee. Garnish with crushed amaretti
cookies and serve immediately. For a more DIY approach
to serving, see notes.

Notes
· If you don't have espresso to use in your affogato,
  strongly brewed coffee is a great substitute. Don't
  be afraid to use instant coffee either in this recipe.
· To keep the ice cream from completely melting, allow
  the espresso to cool a bit before serving.

TIP *When you're planning out your table, place empty platters, boards, and serving dishes on the table when you set it so you know exactly where they'll fit. Remove them before your guests arrive.*

ROAST CHICKEN DINNER

For many of us, the smell of a freshly roasted chicken is a reminder of relaxing nights and home-cooked meals shared with loved ones. Though some people reserve roast chicken for the holidays or special occasions, there is no reason that such a simple yet delicious meal can't be a family dinner staple any night of the week.

One of the great things about comfort foods is that they never go out of style. A meal like roast chicken is a crowd pleaser across a variety of ages and palates. In addition to being a family favorite, roast chicken is also an affordable and easy-to-prepare meal that doesn't require a ton of ingredients or preparation. One quick trip to the grocery store and you're all set.

But having said that, a roast chicken dinner wouldn't be complete without side dishes. Some of our favorites are Cauliflower Gratin, Brown Butter Carrots, and, of course, Sheila's famous Patates. Keep a close eye on the potatoes, as it's not uncommon for someone to try to sneak a bite or two before they're served . . .

TIP *Instead of using plates to serve appetizers, keep it casual and use napkins only. This allows for an easier cleanup and transition to dinner.*

SETTING

When you're setting the table for a comfortable meal, it can be difficult to straddle the line between too casual and too formal. Our approach is to keep things simple but to add one or two subtle accents to give the table a slightly more upscale look.

Start with a crisp white tablecloth, adding light accents of beige and pink. Beige place mats, along with simple flatware and plain white plates, do a fine job of keeping your table well balanced. Light florals, like pale pink and light peach roses, set in small bunches, can bring a touch of elegance to your overall aesthetic without adding too much formality. Consider using an assortment of smaller vases for your florals. They can easily be shifted or shuffled if you need extra table space for the family-style platters.

Also remember that it's important to have a tray to display and easily serve your appetizers. Any tray will do the trick, but we like clear ones, as they will match almost any theme and are tremendously versatile.

If you're looking for a chic way to make the table a bit more special, you can always add place cards to kick things up a notch. We suggest a cute napkin with string or ribbon tied around a painted egg and name card to personalize the setting. Why an egg, you ask? We love finding whimsical ways to spark conversation, especially when hosting guests who may not have met before. What better opening question is there than "What came first: the chicken or the egg?" See page 104 to learn how we paint our eggs, but keep in mind that for a less formal occasion (or to save time) you can skip this step.

To paint your eggs, hard-boil them and allow them to cool completely. Holding the egg on its side, paint one half with a bronze metallic paint. Let it dry for 4-6 minutes, then roll over to expose the other side and repeat.

If you wait until the day before your dinner party to shop for florals, you might find already opened roses on sale!

SEB SAYS *An informal dining table is all about "the more the merrier," so we like to make extra food in case we want to add a guest at the last minute. The worst-case scenario is having lots of delicious leftovers.*

WHAT'S ON THE MENU

As our guests begin to settle in and grab their drinks, we offer nibbles like mixed nuts, marinated olives, chips, and our Seasoned Emmental Snacks, each presented in small bowls. This is a great opportunity to clean out your pantry and put assorted leftover snacks to good use, as you only need small quantities of each. For these small bites, offer toothpicks as flatware and set out a small empty bowl containing a snapped toothpick to show your guests where they can discard used toothpicks.

COURSES

Since roast chicken can make for a heavy meal, we like to start with a smallish appetizer. Vichyssoise Shooters—a chilled potato, leek, and onion soup from Vichy, France, served in a non-traditional way—is a delicious alternative to more traditional appetizers and bridges the gap between the cocktail hour snacks and the main course. We like to serve it in tall shot glasses for easy consumption and cleanup (they take up less space in the dishwasher!), and to save even more time, it can be made a few days in advance and garnished just before serving.

Next, we get into our main course. Instead of individually plating each portion of roast chicken along with the side dishes, we recommend serving everything family-style. It's less demanding on the hosts and allows guests to choose the quantity of each dish themselves. It also makes helping yourself to seconds less awkward!

With a family-style meal it's important to think about positioning when you bring your main course and sides to the table. Some simple planning before your guests arrive can help you allocate enough space to each dish without the table feeling overcrowded.

For dessert we are serving Creamy Baked Pears—a delicious and infrequently used recipe that is sure to have your guests asking for more. You'll be hard pressed to find someone who can't find room for this dessert, even with a stomach full of roast chicken.

If you're entertaining a large group and don't feel like pouring cocktails all night, set up a cocktail station with a charming recipe card for easy self-service.

For casual dinners I like to experiment with new wines, since pairing is less important. I pull out two or three reds and whites so we can sample each one, then we finish those over the course of the next few days.

WHAT'S ON THE BAR

For this meal, we serve a welcoming Bourbon Grapefruit Cocktail with Thyme Simple Syrup. This cocktail is extremely easy to make and pairs beautifully with the small appetizers your guests will nibble on before dinner.

For guests who don't consume alcohol, we suggest offering a non-alcoholic grapefruit spritzer with garnish. It's also easy to make and it can be served as a batch mocktail as well.

Since eventually we will be moving to wines with dinner, our suggestion is to pick your favorite white and red wines, since both are well suited to roast chicken and, given the casual nature of this meal, pairing wines is not necessary.

With bottled water going the way of the dinosaur, we've found that serving tap water in differently shaped and colored bottles makes for an interesting conversation starter. We've used rosé bottles, vodka bottles, and even antique decanters to serve water on the table.

ROAST CHICKEN DINNER

COCKTAILS

BOURBON GRAPEFRUIT COCKTAIL
WITH THYME SIMPLE SYRUP (P112)

NON-ALCOHOLIC GRAPEFRUIT
SPRITZER (P112)

CANAPÉS

SEASONED EMMENTAL SNACKS (P113)

VICHYSSOISE SHOOTERS (P113)

FIRST COURSE

ROAST CHICKEN (P114)

BROWN BUTTER CARROTS (P117)

SHEILA'S PATATES (P117)

CAULIFLOWER GRATIN (P118)

DESSERT

CREAMY BAKED PEARS (P120)

PARTY COUNTDOWN:

ROAST CHICKEN DINNER

3 THREE DAYS BEFORE

○ Send a reminder email or text to your guests with details about the evening.

○ Find some mixed bottles for your water service.

○ Check your inventory of platters, dishes, and shot glasses to make sure you have everything you need.

○ Make your grocery and alcohol list.

○ Grocery shop and stock up at the liquor store.

○ Paint your eggs (see tip on page 104) and assemble the napkin holder name cards.

2 TWO DAYS BEFORE

○ Prepare vegetables like carrots, onions, celery, and cauliflower ahead of time by washing, cutting, and refrigerating in airtight containers.

○ Make the Vichyssoise soup and refrigerate in an airtight container.

TIME- SAVING TIPS

Scale back on side dishes: while we love having a wide variety, you can choose just two if you're pressed for time.

Skip the painted eggs on the place card setting and simply tie the card to the napkin with a piece of string or ribbon.

Change up the dessert. Poach the pears the day before then chop them up and refrigerate in an airtight container. Warm or microwave for 1 minute and serve over plain vanilla ice cream.

1 THE DAY BEFORE

○ Buy flowers, trim them, and place them in water overnight.

○ Take out all your serving platters and dishes, then use sticky notes to keep track of which course is being served in which dish.

○ Cut the emmental cheese into cubes and refrigerate in an airtight container.

0 THE DAY OF

○ Prepare the floral arrangements and set the table.

○ Assemble the seasoned emmental snacks.

○ Set up the bar for your batched cocktails or self-serve cocktail station (add chilled mixes and ice last).

○ Prepare the chickens and refrigerate until they're ready to be roasted.

○ Cut the potatoes and submerge them in cold water to prevent browning until it's time to cook them.

○ Make the brown butter carrots and cauliflower gratin.

○ Prepare the dessert so it is ready to bake after dinner.

○ Take the soup out of the fridge 30 minutes before your guests arrive to allow it to warm to room temperature.

BOURBON
GRAPEFRUIT
COCKTAIL
WITH THYME
SIMPLE SYRUP

COCKTAILS +
SNACKS

BOURBON GRAPEFRUIT COCKTAIL WITH THYME SIMPLE SYRUP

yield: makes 1 cocktail + 3½ cups syrup ·
prep time: 5 minutes + 1 hour to cool ·
cook time: 12 minutes

Ingredients

THYME SIMPLE SYRUP
2 cups granulated sugar
6 thyme sprigs

BOURBON GRAPEFRUIT COCKTAIL
2 oz bourbon
6 Tbsp pink grapefruit juice
1 Tbsp thyme simple syrup
1 pink grapefruit slice, for garnish
1 thyme sprig, for garnish

Method

FOR THE SIMPLE SYRUP
Combine the sugar, thyme, and 2 cups of water in a small saucepan and bring to a boil, without stirring, over medium heat. Reduce the heat to low and simmer, uncovered and without stirring, for 10 minutes. Remove from the heat and let cool for 1 hour. Strain the syrup and refrigerate in an airtight container for up to 3 weeks.

FOR THE COCKTAIL
Fill a cocktail shaker with ice, then add the bourbon, grapefruit juice, and simple syrup. Shake vigorously for 10 seconds. Strain into a rocks glass filled with fresh ice. Garnish with the grapefruit and thyme.

NON-ALCOHOLIC GRAPEFRUIT SPRITZER

yield: makes 1 cocktail · prep time: 5 minutes

Ingredients
½ cup pink grapefruit juice
Splash of Thyme Simple Syrup (see left)
¼ cup sparkling water
1 pink grapefruit slice, for garnish
1 thyme sprig, for garnish

Method
Fill a rocks glass halfway with ice. Pour the grapefruit juice to fill the glass halfway. Add a splash of simple syrup, then fill the remainder of the glass with sparkling water. Garnish with the grapefruit and thyme.

SEASONED EMMENTAL SNACKS

yield: serves 6–8 · prep time: 10 minutes

Ingredients

1 lb emmental cheese, cut in ½-inch cubes
1 Tbsp celery salt

Chips, any flavor
Nuts (almonds and cashews work well)
Olives

Method

In a medium bowl, combine the emmental and celery salt. Gently toss to coat completely. Serve with toothpicks alongside bowls of chips, nuts, and olives.

VICHYSSOISE SHOOTERS

yield: serves 6–8 in bowls, or 16–18 in shot glasses · prep time: 20 minutes · cook time: 30 minutes

Ingredients

1 Tbsp salted butter
1 Tbsp olive oil
1 large leek, white part only, chopped in 1-inch pieces
½ large yellow onion, chopped in 1-inch pieces
2 Yukon gold potatoes, peeled and chopped in 2-inch pieces
1 Tbsp oregano leaves
1 tsp thyme leaves
1 bay leaf
3 cups chicken stock
¼ cup whipping (36%) cream, plus more for garnish (optional)
Sea salt and black pepper
1 Tbsp chopped chives

Method

Melt the butter and the oil in a small stockpot over medium heat. Reduce the heat to medium-low, and add the leeks and the onions.

Cook until the leeks are soft and the onions are translucent, about 8 minutes. Add the potatoes, oregano, thyme, bay leaf, and stock and bring to a boil. Reduce the heat to medium and simmer, uncovered, until the potatoes are tender, about 20 minutes.

Remove from the heat and add the cream. Stir to incorporate then let cool. Once cooled, remove the bay leaf and purée the soup in a blender on high speed until completely smooth. You may need to do this in batches. Once smooth, transfer to a large bowl.

Season the soup to taste with salt and pepper and serve cold or at room temperature in bowls or shot glasses. Garnish each serving with ¼ tsp cream, if desired, then sprinkle with a few chopped chives.

Note

The soup can be stored in an airtight container in the fridge for up to 3 days.

ROAST CHICKEN

yield: serves 6–8 · prep time: 30 minutes + 15 minutes to rest · cook time: 1 hour

Ingredients

CHICKEN

2 (each 3 lb) chickens

4 Tbsp salted butter, divided

6 thyme sprigs, divided

4 rosemary sprigs, divided

4 Tbsp olive oil, divided

Kosher salt and black pepper

3 stalks celery, chopped in
    1-inch pieces

2 carrots, peeled and
    chopped in 1-inch pieces

4 garlic cloves

2 bay leaves

4 cups chicken stock,
    plus more for jus

JUS

1 Tbsp cornstarch

4 cups roasting pan juices

Kosher salt and black pepper

Method

FOR THE CHICKEN

Preheat the oven to 375°F. Remove the chicken giblets, any excess fat, and leftover pin feathers and pat dry.

Place each chicken breast side up with its legs facing you. Gently slide your fingers under the skin to loosen, being careful not to tear the skin. Rub the butter under the skin.

Place 1 sprig each of thyme and rosemary in the cavity of each chicken.

Place each chicken in a medium bowl. Rub with the oil and season with salt and pepper.

With each chicken still breast side up and legs facing you, truss it with kitchen twine to secure the legs together and the wings to the body of the bird. (There are some great YouTube videos available online to show you how to do this.)

In a roasting pan large enough to hold both chickens snugly without crowding, mix together the celery, carrots, garlic, bay leaves, and stock. Add the remaining rosemary and thyme.

Place the chickens on top of the vegetables. Roast, uncovered, for 30 minutes, then baste each chicken with the roasting pan juices every 15 minutes until the internal temperature reaches 165°F in the center of the breast. This should take about 1 hour, but check the temperature with a meat thermometer to be sure.

Remove the chickens from the baking dish and transfer to a platter to rest for 15 minutes before serving.

Strain the roasting pan juices, reserving the liquid to make the jus.

FOR THE JUS

Whisk the cornstarch in 3 Tbsp of cold water until completely combined to make a slurry. Set aside.

Place the roasting pan juices in a medium saucepan and bring to a boil over medium-high heat. You may want to add some stock to increase the yield.

Reduce the heat to medium, add the cornstarch slurry and cook, stirring frequently, until the jus is thickened enough to coat the back of a spoon. Season to taste with salt and pepper. Serve warm alongside the chicken.

SHEILA'S PATATES

| SEB SAYS |

*Why do we use the
French name for
potatoes? Well, the
recipe comes from my
French mother, and
my brother and I grew
up calling these by
their French name.
Even today our entire
family still calls
them patates.*

BROWN BUTTER CARROTS

yield: serves 6–8 · prep time: 20 minutes · cook time: 25 minutes

Ingredients

**2 bunches field carrots
    (12–16 carrots)**
2 Tbsp olive oil
½ cup butter
Kosher salt and black pepper

Method

Preheat the oven to 375°F. Line a baking sheet with parchment paper.

Trim the carrot greens down to 2 inches and scrub the carrots to remove any dirt. Pat dry with paper towel and place on the prepared baking sheet.

Drizzle the carrots with the oil and dot with pats of the butter. Season to taste with salt and pepper.

Bake, turning after 10 minutes to coat evenly with butter, until slightly caramelized and easily pierced with a fork, 25 minutes.

SHEILA'S PATATES

yield: serves 6–8 · prep time: 15 minutes · cook time: 30 minutes

Ingredients

½ cup canola oil
1 cup butter
3 lb baby new potatoes, washed and quartered
Kosher salt and black pepper

Method

Warm a large nonstick skillet over medium-high heat, then add the oil and butter. Once the butter has melted, add the potatoes and stir to coat.

Reduce the heat to medium and cook, stirring occasionally, until the potatoes are golden and cooked through, about 30 minutes. Season to taste with salt and pepper and serve warm.

CAULIFLOWER GRATIN

yield: serves 6–8 · prep time: 30 minutes · cook time: 25–30 minutes

Ingredients

BÉCHAMEL SAUCE

½ cup butter

1 large shallot, finely diced

2 garlic cloves, minced

½ cup all-purpose flour

2 cups milk, room temperature

½ cup whipping (36%) cream, room temperature

Ground nutmeg

Dry mustard powder

Ground cloves

½ cup grated parmigiano-reggiano cheese

CAULIFLOWER

2 medium cauliflowers, cut into large florets

1 cup shredded cheddar cheese

1 cup shredded Swiss cheese

¼ cup shaved parmigiano-reggiano cheese

Black pepper

Method

FOR THE BÉCHAMEL SAUCE

Warm a small saucepan over medium heat, then melt the butter. Add the shallots and garlic and cook until soft, about 3 minutes.

Stir in the flour and cook, stirring continuously, until light brown and bubbling, about 1 minute. Slowly add the milk and cream, again whisking continuously to prevent lumps. Add a pinch of nutmeg, a pinch of mustard powder, and ½ pinch of cloves.

Increase the heat to medium-high to bring to a simmer. Cook, stirring continuously, until thickened, about 1 minute. Remove from the heat and stir in the parmigiano-reggiano until melted.

FOR THE CAULIFLOWER

Preheat the oven to 350°F. Bring a large pot of salted water to a boil over high heat. Prepare an ice bath.

Cook the cauliflower in the boiling water until fork-tender, about 3 minutes. Immediately transfer to the ice bath to stop the cooking process. Drain and set aside.

In a small bowl, combine the three cheeses.

Place half of the cauliflower in a shallow baking dish just large enough to hold everything snugly but without crowding, then pour half of the béchamel over-top. Sprinkle with half of the cheese blend. Add the remaining cauliflower, top with the remaining béchamel, and season with pepper. Bake until the top of the cauliflower is golden brown and the bechamel is bubbling, about 15 minutes.

Sprinkle the remaining cheese over the cauliflower, set the oven to broil, and bake until golden, 3–4 minutes. Watch carefully to avoid burning.

CREAMY BAKED PEARS

yield: serves 6 · prep time: 10 minutes · cook time: 25 minutes

Ingredients

½ cup butter, divided

2 Tbsp granulated sugar, divided

3 Bosc pears, skin on, halved
   and cored

1 cup whipping (36%) cream

Method

Preheat the oven to 375°F. Grease a shallow baking dish just large enough to hold the pears snugly without crowding with 2 Tbsp of the butter and sprinkle with 1 Tbsp of the sugar.

Place the pear halves in the baking dish, cut sides down. Rub the remaining butter over the pears and sprinkle with the remaining sugar.

Bake for 10 minutes. Remove from the oven and pour the cream into the baking dish. Return to the oven and bake until the pears are soft, about 15 minutes. Serve warm.

2

A LITTLE
MORE
EFFORT

SPRING LUNCHEON

The arrival of spring is a marker not only of warmer weather but of outdoor hosting as well. We feel genuine relief that the colder months have passed and we can finally organize get-togethers in our backyard or by the lake. As the early blooms start to appear, the thought of lighter, brighter meals—and fewer layers—gets us excited about seeing the friends we've missed over the last few months, separated by our differing winter activities. Some have searched out warmer climates, while others embraced the cold on the slopes or sat by the fire. But when spring arrives, we embrace the opportunity to come back together.

Our spring lunch features dishes that burst with color and flavor, and bright, airy décor elements that immediately lift your spirits as you reconnect and begin to make plans for the summer months. So, let's get things started, enjoy the abundance of fresh ingredients, break out some crisp cocktails, and enjoy a meal that celebrates all that is spring!

TIP *We find hosting a lunch is a great alternative to hosting a dinner party for several reasons. First, our nights get booked up so quickly between work and family commitments that a lunch feels like a nice change and an opportunity to get away from the default of entertaining only in the evenings. Second, we can vary the menu with lighter items. And third, it allows for an early cleanup so we can have a restful evening.*

SEB SAYS *Sheila and I are big fans of chargers to ground the setting. A charger is an oversized plate that fits under the main dish and can either remain on the table for the entire meal or serve as the plate for the shared main courses.*

Try mixing up the courses between individually plated items and sharing platters—it reduces the amount of work, so you can spend more time with your guests.

SETTING

The setting for a spring lunch starts with a crisp white linen table decorated with bunches of fresh tulips in assorted colors. Tulips are the perfect choice for your spring arrangement given the multitude of colors readily available and the fact that they are relatively inexpensive. Using a variety of differently shaped and styled vases gives your table an eclectic look and allows you to make use of all those vases you have stacked in the cupboard above the fridge! We like to keep to one color of tulip per vase, but you can mix all the tulips together and have multicolored bunches if you prefer. In either case, having at least three or four different colors will offer enough variation to give your table that pop it needs.

For the individual place settings, use a pastel-colored napkin, folded into a narrow rectangle, onto which you can tie a ribbon in an accent color. Place a personalized place card overtop for a touch of elegance. If possible, buy an extra bunch of white tulips and slip one into each place setting to continue the tulip theme—just remember to add them right before your guests arrive so they're as fresh as possible.

When your guests are seated, let them know that they can pull the tulip from their setting and place it in one of the center vases. And when it's time to go home, they can make little tulip bundles from the centerpieces and tie them with the place card ribbon.

For dishware, we like to use white, glass, and light pastel dishes, which provide a complementary backdrop to the bright foods we serve. Mixing and matching is completely fine, and in fact, we would even encourage it.

TIP

You may think it's an old wives' tale, but dropping a penny in the water with your tulips really does keep the stems from wilting too quickly and extends the life of the tulips.

WHAT'S ON THE MENU

When our guests arrive, we serve bite-sized colorful canapés, also sometimes called hors d'oeuvres, that feature fresh ingredients that scream "Spring is here!" We've got Blackberry + Bocconcini Skewers with Basil + Balsamic Glaze, Strawberry Mango Salsa Cups, and, Seb's personal favorite, Spring Chicken Salad on Green Apple Slices. We like to keep each canapé on its own tray. Not only does this look cleaner, but it also allows guests who may not like an ingredient to simply avoid that tray.

COURSES

For our lunch course, we focus on lighter dishes that can be served at room temperature or cold—a nice departure from those "stick-to-your-ribs" courses that we enjoy over the winter months. We also choose dishes that match our décor, with a heavy emphasis on pastel colors, which are ideally suited to the time of year.

What better way to start the seated portion of a meal than Creamy Spring Pea Soup with Sprouts to embrace the fresh flavors and bright colors of the season? While the ingredient list is lengthy, the recipe is simple and can be made a few days in advance. On the day of your lunch party, you just have to finish it with a drizzle of cream and pinch of micro herbs.

Our salad course is inspired by a spring garden brimming with blooms. While the mixed leaves combine different textures and colors of lettuces, it's the cucumber wrap, dressing, and orange segments that really make this course a feast for the eyes and the palate.

Although the soup and salad can be individually plated, we like to serve the salmon entrée on a large platter so we can avoid going back and forth to the kitchen. It also looks great on the table with the lemon slices, parsley, and dill—another example of pastel colors that tie into our décor. To accompany the salmon, we quickly blanch then season some crisp green beans onto which we sprinkle some toasted almonds. Again, this is a dish that is equally good warm, at room temperature, or chilled.

Finally, instead of a full dessert, we like to serve cookies or something light. We've borrowed a recipe from our good friend Sally Doerge for this book. We've marveled at her Famously Spicy + Chewy Ginger Cookies for years and finally, after much pleading, she gave in and shared the recipe with us!

WHAT'S ON THE BAR

When it comes to spring cocktails, as with the food, it's all about color!

A batched cocktail like our Pink Lemonade Rosé is fresh, crisp, and delicious but also relatively low in alcohol (and can even be made alcohol-free if you use white cranberry juice instead of rosé). Your guests can help themselves, saving you from constantly bartending.

As for the Prosecco Margarita, this easy-to-make cocktail is sure to be a big hit with any tequila lovers in the crowd. It provides a perfect balance of flavor between the sweetness of the simple syrup, the crisp prosecco, and the tart lime juice.

SPRING LUNCHEON

COCKTAILS

PROSECCO MARGARITA (P132)

PINK LEMONADE ROSÉ (P132)

CANAPÉS

STRAWBERRY MANGO SALSA CUPS (P136)

SPRING CHICKEN SALAD ON GREEN APPLE SLICES (P137)

BLACKBERRY + BOCCONCINI SKEWERS WITH BASIL + BALSAMIC GLAZE (P137)

FIRST COURSE

CREAMY SPRING PEA SOUP WITH SPROUTS (P139)

SECOND COURSE

CUCUMBER SALAD ROLL WITH ORANGES, SUNFLOWER SEEDS + HONEY MUSTARD VINAIGRETTE (P140)

THIRD COURSE

OVEN-POACHED SALMON WITH DILL SAUCE (P143)

GREEN BEANS WITH TOASTED ALMONDS (P144)

DESSERT

SALLY'S FAMOUSLY SPICY + CHEWY GINGER COOKIES (P147)

PARTY COUNTDOWN:

SPRING LUNCHEON

3 THREE DAYS BEFORE

- ○ Send a reminder email or text to your guests with details about the lunch.

- ○ Make your grocery and alcohol lists.

- ○ Check you have enough plates and glasses for your guests.

2 TWO DAYS BEFORE

- ○ Grocery shop and stock up at the liquor store.

- ○ Buy flowers, trim them, and place them in water overnight.

- ○ Make the soup and refrigerate in an airtight container.

- ○ Make the salad dressing and refrigerate in an airtight container.

TIME-SAVING TIPS

Skip the canapés.

Drop one of the specialty cocktails and replace it with a white wine spritzer (white wine and sparkling water or soda).

Instead of wrapping the salad with a cucumber ribbon, use 2 cucumber ribbons to make a circle on the plate, then fill it with the salad.

Buy pre-made phyllo or savory pastry cups instead of making your own.

1 THE DAY BEFORE

○ Prepare the floral arrangements, set the table, and build the napkin settings (without tulips).

○ Make the chicken salad and refrigerate in an airtight container.

○ Make the salsa and refrigerate in an airtight container.

○ Make the skewers and refrigerate in an airtight container.

○ Bake the ginger cookies and store at room temperature in an airtight container.

0 THE DAY OF

○ Assemble the salad bouquets and keep them wrapped on a tray in the fridge.

○ Marinate and dress the salmon.

○ Partially mix the batch cocktails (hold off on adding ice or sparkling water and prosecco until right before guests arrive).

PROSECCO MARGARITA

yield: makes 1 cocktail · prep time: 3 minutes

Ingredients

1 oz tequila
½ oz triple sec
2 Tbsp simple syrup (page 11)
2 Tbsp lime juice
3 oz prosecco or sparkling wine
1 lime slice

Method

Place the tequila, triple sec, simple syrup, and lime juice in a cocktail shaker, add ice, and shake vigorously. Strain into a tall martini glass or champagne flute, then top with prosecco. Garnish with the lime.

PINK LEMONADE ROSÉ

yield: makes 24 cocktails · prep time: 3 minutes

Ingredients

2 (each 10 fl oz) packs frozen pink lemonade concentrate
2 (each 750 ml) bottles pale rosé
3 (each 26 fl oz) bottles sparkling water
½ cup lemon juice, divided (6–8 lemons)
1 small tin pink sugar sprinkles
8 lemons, cut in slices
Edible flowers, optional

Method

Place the lemonade concentrate in a punch bowl (if you don't have a punch bowl, any attractive bowl large enough to hold all the ingredients will work). Add the wine and 2 bottles of the sparkling water. Stir in ¼ cup of the lemon juice.

Spread a large amount of the sprinkles in a shallow bowl, about ¼-inch deep. Place the remaining ¼ cup of lemon juice in a narrow bowl.

Set aside 24 lemon slices for garnish.

Just before your guests arrive, add the remaining sparkling water to the punch bowl and fill it with ice. Stir well and add the remaining lemon slices.

To assemble, place the rim of a glass in the lemon juice and then roll in the sugar to coat. Pour the lemonade into the sugar-coated glass and garnish with a lemon slice and edible flowers (if using).

When you're making batch cocktails, don't splurge on high-end alcohols. A decent tequila and rosé will do just fine when mixed with ingredients like pink lemonade.

BLACKBERRY +
BOCCONCINI
SKEWERS WITH BASIL
+ BALSAMIC GLAZE

CANAPÉS

STRAWBERRY MANGO SALSA CUPS

yield: serves 6–8 · prep time: 15 minutes ·
cook time: 10 minutes

Ingredients

PHYLLO CUPS
3 (18- x 14-inch) sheets frozen phyllo, thawed
¼ cup olive oil
Sea salt and black pepper

STRAWBERRY MANGO SALSA
6 strawberries, diced small
2 Tbsp small-diced mango
1 Tbsp small-diced red onion
1 tsp small-diced jalapeño, seeds and veins removed
¼ tsp black pepper
1 Tbsp grapeseed oil
2 tsp lime juice
2 tsp honey
Sea salt
¼ cup mashed ripe avocado
6 cilantro leaves, finely chopped

Method

FOR THE PHYLLO CUPS
Preheat the oven to 350°F.

Cut the phyllo sheets lengthwise so you end up with six sheets that each measure 9- x 14-inches. Then lay a single phyllo sheet flat and brush it entirely with oil. Place a second sheet evenly over the first, pat it down, and brush again with oil. Repeat for a total of six layers. Season the top layer with a pinch of salt and pepper, then cut the layered sheets into approximately 3-inch squares. You should wind up with 12 layered squares.

Press the phyllo layers into a mini muffin tray, one stack per cup, and bake until the edges are golden, about 10 minutes. (Pour some water into any empty muffin cups to prevent burning.) Allow to cool at room temperature and store in an airtight container for up to 1 week.

FOR THE SALSA
Mix together the strawberries, mangos, onions, jalapeños, and pepper in a medium bowl. Add the oil, lime juice, honey, and salt to taste. Mix well and set aside.

Remove the phyllo cups from the muffin pan and, using two small spoons, add 1 tsp of avocado to each one. Top with the strawberry mango salsa and garnish with a sprinkle of cilantro. Serve immediately, as the phyllo will go soggy if these sit for too long.

SPRING CHICKEN SALAD ON GREEN APPLE SLICES

yield: serves 6–8 · prep time: 30 minutes

Ingredients

2 medium-sized green apples
2 Tbsp lemon juice mixed with 1 cup water
1 cooked chicken breast, shredded
12 green grapes, quartered
¼ cup diced celery
2 Tbsp roughly chopped dried cranberries
2 Tbsp walnut pieces, toasted
1 Tbsp coarsely chopped flat-leaf parsley
1 Tbsp lemon juice
1 tsp grainy Dijon mustard
¼ cup brick-style cream cheese, softened
¼ cup mayonnaise
Sea salt and white pepper
1 Tbsp chopped chives

Method

Slice the apples crosswise into ½-inch disks and cut half-circle shapes on either side of the core. Place the slices in the lemon water and set aside.

In a medium bowl, mix together the chicken, grapes, celery, cranberries, walnuts, parsley, lemon juice, and Dijon.

Mix together the cream cheese and mayonnaise and stir into the chicken mixture until evenly combined. Season to taste with salt and pepper.

Remove the apple slices from the lemon-water mixture and pat dry with a paper towel.

Place 1 tsp of the chicken mixture on each apple slice and sprinkle with chives for garnish.

Note

This recipe will yield enough chicken for 12–16 canapés, but if you only make 12, you'll have enough topping left over for a chicken salad sandwich the next day!

BLACKBERRY + BOCCONCINI SKEWERS WITH BASIL + BALSAMIC GLAZE

yield: serves 6–8 · prep time: 15 minutes

Ingredients

12–16 cocktail-size bocconcini balls
1 tsp olive oil
1 tsp grated orange zest
12 (4- to 5-inch-long) skewers
12 basil leaves, washed and dried
½ pint blackberries
Balsamic glaze
Sea salt

Method

Pat the bocconcini balls dry with a paper towel, then transfer to a bowl. Add the oil and orange zest and stir to evenly coat the bocconcini. Place a cheese ball about one-third of the way up a skewer. Fold a basil leaf and place it on the skewer. Insert the skewer into the stem end of a blackberry. Repeat with the remaining skewers.

Drizzle the skewers with balsamic glaze and sprinkle with salt before serving.

CREAMY SPRING PEA SOUP WITH SPROUTS

yield: serves 6–8 · prep time: 30 minutes + 2–48 hours to chill · cook time: 15–20 minutes

Ingredients

⅓ cup butter
½ cup diced white onion
⅓ cup sliced leeks
1 tsp dry mustard powder
½ tsp sweet paprika
2½ cups vegetable stock
1¼ cups whipping (36%) cream, divided
2 cups frozen green peas, thawed
½ cup baby spinach leaves
½ cup baby arugula
1 Tbsp mint leaves
1 Tbsp tarragon leaves
Kosher salt and black pepper
Micro sprouts, for garnish

Method

In a small stockpot, melt the butter over medium heat, then add the onions and leeks. Reduce the heat to medium-low and sweat until the onions are translucent and the leeks are soft, about 8 minutes. Stir occasionally to avoid browning.

Stir in the mustard powder, paprika, stock, and 1 cup of the cream. Bring to a boil, then reduce the heat and simmer, uncovered and without stirring, for 5 minutes. Add the peas, remove from the heat, and let cool to room temperature.

Once cool, transfer to a blender. Add the spinach, arugula, mint, and tarragon, and purée until smooth. You'll need to do this in batches, as a blender should never be more than two-thirds full. Keep in mind that the greens and herbs will need to be roughly portioned into each batch. (You can also use a large bowl and immersion blender for this. Watch for splashing, though.)

Combine all the batches in a single large bowl, then season to taste with salt and pepper and refrigerate in an airtight container for up to 48 hours (or a minimum of 2 hours). Serve chilled with a drizzle of cream and a pinch of micro sprouts.

TIP

Teacups make an unexpected and whimsical serving vessel for the soup. These little touches can wow your guests without much additional effort on your part.

CUCUMBER SALAD ROLL WITH ORANGES, SUNFLOWER SEEDS + HONEY MUSTARD VINAIGRETTE

yield: serves 6 · prep time: 30 minutes · cook time: 5 minutes

Ingredients

HONEY MUSTARD VINAIGRETTE

¼ cup liquid honey

¼ cup lemon juice

¼ cup orange juice

1 Tbsp grainy Dijon mustard

1 tsp Garlic Confit (page 164)
   or garlic-infused olive oil

1 cup grapeseed oil

SALAD

1 Tbsp kosher salt

18 asparagus spears

3 cups mixed spring greens

3 cups baby kale

½ head radicchio, core removed,
   cut in ½-inch strips

1 English cucumber, ends trimmed

1 small bunch chives

2 to 3 oranges, peeled and
   segmented (24 segments)

¼ cup sunflower seeds

Sea salt and black pepper

Method

FOR THE DRESSING

Place the honey, lemon and orange juices, Dijon, and garlic confit in a blender. Blend on medium speed, slowly drizzling in the oil until combined. Refrigerate in an airtight container for up to 1 week.

FOR THE SALAD

Bring a large pot of hot water to a boil over high heat, then add the kosher salt. Prepare an ice bath and set aside.

Wash the asparagus. Snap off and discard the tough ends. Place the asparagus in the boiling water for 2 minutes (thicker asparagus may need to cook for longer), then immediately transfer to the ice bath.

Combine the mixed greens, baby kale, and radicchio in a bowl and set aside.

Slice the cucumber in half lengthwise, and, using a mandolin, cut it into six long, thin ribbons and reserve the rest for another use. We like to cut the remaining cucumbers into slices and serve lightly salted with the canapés. Lay a cucumber strip vertically perpendicular to the edge of the counter. Spread about 1 cup of the greens crosswise onto the cucumber (the greens will be parallel with the edge of the counter) and place 4 chives across them. Try to center the greens on the cucumber. Lay 3 asparagus spears on top of the greens.

Holding the greens in place, roll the cucumber up and around the greens to secure the ingredients and lay it flat with the ends of the cucumber ribbon on the bottom, underneath the greens. You can use a toothpick to hold everything in place until you're ready to serve.

If you're not serving these immediately, cover them with a damp cloth and refrigerate for up to 2 hours. Place the salad roll in the center of a plate and arrange 4 orange segments around it, then top each salad with 2 tsp of sunflower seeds, 2 Tbsp of dressing, and a pinch of sea salt and black pepper. You can use the remaining dressing over the green beans (see page 144).

Note

If you don't have a mandolin, carefully cut the cucumber with a knife. Or, instead of wrapping the salad in a cucumber ribbon, you can place the greens in the center of the plate and garnish with cucumber ribbons sliced with a vegetable peeler.

OVEN-POACHED SALMON WITH DILL SAUCE

yield: serves 6–8 · prep time: 30 minutes · cook time: 30 minutes

Ingredients

SALMON

2 shallots, thinly sliced

¼ fennel bulb, julienned

1 (4-inch) piece leek (white portion only), sliced into thin rounds

1 stalk celery, thinly sliced diagonally

½ tsp thyme leaves

4 lemons, divided

1 (2 lb) salmon fillet, center cut, skin and pin bones removed

¼ cup fish or vegetable stock

¼ cup dry white wine

½ cup flat-leaf parsley leaves

2 Tbsp dill leaves

Sea salt and black pepper

3 Tbsp olive oil

DILL SAUCE

½ cup plain Greek yogurt

½ cup plain yogurt

½ cup brick-style cream cheese

1 Tbsp olive oil

4 mint leaves, chopped

1 Tbsp dill leaves, chopped

1 tsp black pepper

½ tsp sea salt

1 tsp grated lemon zest (from lemon used in the salmon)

2 tsp lemon juice (from lemon used in the salmon)

Method

FOR THE SALMON

Preheat the oven to 350°F. Line a 9- x 13-inch baking tray with parchment paper, pressing it into the corners and making sure the parchment hangs over the edges of the tray by about 3 inches.

Arrange the shallots, fennel, leeks, celery, and thyme on the parchment. Using a vegetable peeler, peel 8 strips of zest from one of the lemons and add them to the dish. Reserve the remaining lemon zest and juice for the dill sauce. Place the salmon overtop of the vegetables. Pour the stock and wine over the fish. Cut 2 of the remaining lemons into 4 wedges each.

Cut a 9- x 13-inch piece of parchment and place it over the fish, weighing down the edges with the lemon wedges.

Bake until the center of the salmon is firm to the touch and the internal temperature is 135°F, 30 minutes. You can peel back the parchment to test the internal temperature or simply pierce the parchment with a sharp temperature probe.

Carefully remove the lemon quarters, then the top sheet of parchment paper, and allow the salmon to cool slightly. Be careful. There will be a lot of steam.

The salmon can be stored at room temperature for up to 3 hours or refrigerated overnight if you're making it ahead.

Using a long offset spatula or barbecue spatula, transfer the salmon to a serving platter (discard the vegetables and spices). Cut the remaining lemon into rounds and garnish the salmon with lemon rounds, parsley, dill, salt, and pepper, and then drizzle with the oil.

FOR THE SAUCE

Mix together the yogurts, cream cheese, and oil. Stir in the mint, dill, pepper, salt, and lemon zest and juice. Serve in a small bowl alongside the salmon. Refrigerate in an airtight container for up to 1 week.

GREEN BEANS WITH TOASTED ALMONDS

yield: serves 6–8 · prep time: 10 minutes · cook time: 2 minutes

Ingredients

1 Tbsp kosher salt

1 lb green beans, trimmed

Sea salt and black pepper

¼ cup sliced almonds, toasted

**Cucumber Salad Roll dressing
(page 140)**

Method

Bring a large pot of hot water to a boil over high heat and add the kosher salt. Prepare an ice bath.

Place the beans in the boiling water until they are crisp and bright green, 60–90 seconds (thicker beans may require longer), immediately transfer to the ice bath for 15–20 seconds, then drain. The ice bath will prevent the beans from continuing to cook.

Arrange the beans in a shallow serving dish large enough to hold them snugly without crowding, season to taste with salt and pepper, and sprinkle with the almonds.

Drizzle the dressing overtop and serve chilled or at room temperature.

SALLY'S FAMOUSLY SPICY + CHEWY GINGER COOKIES

yield: makes 18 cookies · prep time: 20 minutes + 30 minutes–overnight to chill · cook time: 12–16 minutes

Ingredients

2½ cups all-purpose flour

2¼ tsp baking soda

½ tsp table salt

1 Tbsp ground ginger

½ tsp black pepper

½ tsp ground allspice

¼ tsp ground cinnamon

¼ tsp ground cloves

¼ tsp ground nutmeg

¾ cup butter

½ cup granulated sugar,
    plus extra for rolling

½ cup packed brown sugar

1 large egg

1 Tbsp freshly grated ginger

¼ cup dark molasses

1 Tbsp coarse sea salt

Method

In a medium bowl, mix together the flour, baking soda, and salt. Mix in the ground ginger, pepper, allspice, cinnamon, cloves, and nutmeg. Set aside.

In a stand mixer fitted with the paddle attachment, beat the butter on high speed with both sugars, the egg, and fresh ginger until light and fluffy, 4–5 minutes.

Turn the mixer to low speed. Slowly add the molasses, then the flour mixture, and mix until fully combined.

Roll the dough into a single large ball, then wrap in plastic wrap and freeze for at least 30 minutes, or preferably overnight.

Preheat the oven to 350°F. Line two baking sheets with parchment paper.

Remove the dough ball from the freezer and allow to soften slightly, about 15 minutes. Pour some more granulated sugar into a small bowl. Divide the dough into 18 evenly sized balls, wet your hands, and roll each ball in the sugar. Work quickly, as the dough needs to remain chilled.

Place the balls about 4 inches apart on the baking sheets and sprinkle each one with a pinch of sea salt.

Place one baking sheet on the top rack of your oven and the other on the bottom rack and bake the cookies for 6–8 minutes. Rotate the sheets and bake until brown, 6–8 minutes.

Place the cookies on a wire rack to cool for 20 minutes, then transfer to an airtight container for up to 5 days (although they are so good, they won't last that long).

Note

The dough can be rolled into balls and frozen, so you can bake up some of these ginger delights whenever the urge strikes.

WINTER WARM-UP

Although we are a family of beach-lovers, there is something magical about getting together with our friends for a warm and cozy winter evening. When the mercury plummets or the ground is covered in snow, it's difficult to not feel full of joy sitting by a roaring fire with a group of special people.

One of our favorite things about entertaining in the winter is hosting on a weekend when no one has to rush off anywhere. We usually invite everyone to come a little earlier than normal since it gets dark so early and we can space out the courses, which helps when you are serving a heavier-style menu.

A weekend evening of casual entertaining indoors also lends itself to a real time-out where we turn off our phones, or even just turn the ringers to silent, live in the moment, and maybe have an impromptu game of chess, backgammon, or charades.

While the main point of a winter warm-up dinner is for you and your guests to be comfy and relaxed, this doesn't mean preparing only simple recipes. Especially on a weekend, you may find yourself doing the opposite, as you have more time to prep. But rest assured that many of the dishes in this chapter can cook in the background while you and your guests relax. The aromas of the rich, decadent courses will fill your home, creating the perfect atmosphere for a long evening of great conversation. If you're still a bit wary of hosting, the recipes in this chapter may seem intimidating, but you'll be able to do a lot of work in advance so that you have a stress-free winter meal.

Whether it's a formal Christmas Eve, a relaxed Christmas Day, or just an excuse to gather your favorite group of people together, our winter warm-up menu will fit any occasion!

SEB SAYS *We love to start the evening all gathered together with any appetizers served family-style to allow guests to catch up and socialize before sitting down for dinner. This is when the family backgammon rivalries usually ramp up in our house!*

TIP *A fresh piece of garland can last the whole season if stored properly. Not only is it a great centerpiece for winter meals, but it can also be used on outdoor tables in the fall before winter arrives. Store it in a cool place like the garage, or wrap it in a plastic bag and store in the fridge if you have room, misting it lightly every few days.*

SETTING

While most of our table settings start with a crisp tablecloth, this winter warm-up is a little different. For this occasion, we use lots of wood and greenery, and subtle touches of lighting to give the table a glow. A wooden table makes an ideal base if you have one. Lay a long garland down the center of the table and scatter mini tea light candles at intervals for ambient lighting. Rather than resting your plateware directly on the table, we recommend using wooden charger plates at each place setting to avoid any scratches or spills. If you don't have a wooden table, use a beige or brown tablecloth instead.

Despite this relatively formal table setting, we encourage you to host your guests in a more casual area of your home before seating them for dinner—somewhere they can socialize, enjoy canapés, and settle into a deep sofa or armchair. We like to build a fire in our living room and let the crackling set the mood. Even though this is one of our more structured dinner parties, we put out a couple of fur blankets to encourage our guests to get comfortable before we move to the table or, in some cases, retreat for dessert.

When you're preparing a dinner like this one, it's a nice touch to give your guests an idea of what's on the menu by having a printed menu at each place setting. There's no need to go all out when printing the menu—a simple, minimalist design is more than enough. Printed menus are a lost art that elevate the evening with very little effort.

Another easy way to take your table setting up a notch is to use pomegranates for place cards. Whether you choose to write directly on the pomegranate or stick a name card on the top of it, this chic DIY project is sure to add an extra element to your décor.

Laurie

Tessa

Emily

Tom

MENU

I

French Grinotes, Gougères & Baked Brie
winter cocktails and martinis

II

Stuffed and Baked Tomato
bechamel cheese sauce, black forest ham, white wine

III

Classic Boeuf Bourguinon
parisian double-whipped potatoes, fall root vegetables,
peark onions and parsley

IV

Vanilla Ice Cream with Warm Chocolate Sauce
roasted stone fruit

SHEILA SAYS *Early in the holiday season I always go out and buy a garland long enough for our dining room table and then place it on the fireplace mantel or somewhere else in our living room. I move it to the table when we're hosting dinners throughout the month. While the garland will dry out faster than if you were to store it in a cool spot between uses, this is a great way to repurpose one holiday décor piece for multiple events and it will still last two or more weeks.*

WHAT'S ON THE MENU

The easiest way to make your winter warm-up run as smoothly as possible is by preparing as much as possible ahead of time. The whole point of hosting your friends and family for dinner is to catch up and socialize, and neither you nor your guests will be relaxed if you're in the kitchen frantically preparing dishes all night. In an effort to prevent the "chaos in the kitchen" scenario, we've suggested three canapés for this meal that can be made ahead of time and should be ready to serve as your guests arrive.

The first canapé is slices of baguette with a variety of spreads. While we have many spreads to choose from, the three that work best for this meal are Duck Rillette, Garlic Confit, and Herbed Chèvre. The recipes for these spreads aren't difficult but they do have multiple steps and take time, so we recommend making them a day or so in advance and letting them rest in the fridge until the big night.

To complement the baguette and spreads we have a Cranberry Baked Brie and Gougères. Baked brie is the perfect blank canvas to showcase a variety of toppings. Get creative or use whatever you have in your kitchen to make this dish your own. Our favorite additions are fresh seasonal fruit, sundried tomatoes, honey, walnuts, and grapes.

As your guests finish their cocktails and slowly move on from the delicious canapés, it's time to start the seated portion of the meal. The first course will make you feel like you just came in from skiing: Ham + Béchamel Baked Tomatoes. This classic winter dish is easy to prepare and fits effortlessly into our winter theme. Not only is it a delicious way to begin your meal, but when prepared correctly it also looks pretty similar to a classic red Christmas ornament if you happen to be entertaining over the holidays!

Next, we get into our main course. When you picture the perfect winter meal up at a chalet, you'd be hard pressed to find a better-fitting main course than Boeuf Bourguignon. While it does require some work, it will have your guests' mouths watering for weeks afterward as they beg you for the recipe.

Since Boeuf Bourguignon is such a heavy dish and roast vegetables are mixed in with it, we recommend not overwhelming your guests with too many sides. A single side dish that always goes well with beef is Parisian-Styled Mashed Potatoes, or Pommes Purée. While some people may prefer to keep their meat and potatoes separate, we love to have them in the same bowl to allow the meat juices to mix in with the potatoes.

And then it's time for the classic Cheese Course. The number of cheeses we like to offer depends on how many people we're hosting, but as a basic rule, we aim to have at least 1½ oz per person and a minimum of three cheeses to choose from. We like to cover all the main categories, including cow's milk cheese, sheep's milk cheese, and goat's milk cheese. Specific favorites of ours include brie, camembert, reblochon, tomme de savoie, caprice des dieux, chèvre, and tomme des Pyrénées. You can serve a cheese board and allow guests to help themselves but to add a touch of formality we sometimes like to make individual mini cheese plates for each guest.

Finally, we are offering a super simple dessert of vanilla ice cream with dark chocolate sauce. Dame Blanche is one of the most universally loved winter desserts and is sure to be a hit regardless of how full your guests may be at this point. The name of this easy-to-make dessert comes from an old French tale. The story goes that a ghost named Dame Blanche would block a bridge in Normandy and that only those who stopped to dance with her would be allowed to pass. Seb's mom used to tell him and his brother this story as they enjoyed their ice cream and chocolate sauce. We've also included a separate recipe for baked stone fruit that can be added to the dessert, or enjoyed with vanilla ice cream only.

WHAT'S ON THE BAR

It's winter, and what goes better with that cold air than martinis?

The first cocktail we recommend for your winter evening is an Espresso Martini. It offers a richer alternative to the other two cocktails and also provides a little pick-me-up early in the evening. Rest assured, though, that it won't keep you awake all night the way an espresso at the end of a meal might!

Then, we move to the fan-favorite Cosmopolitan. This classic cocktail is perfect to sip on by the fire as you nibble on canapés and socialize with your guests. All you need to make a Cosmo is vodka, cranberry juice, and Cointreau.

If cranberry juice and Cointreau aren't your thing, try replacing them with dry vermouth and some olives to create a Classic Martini. More traditional than the Cosmopolitan, a Classic Martini is a welcome sight to most as it can be mixed with either vodka or gin. Make sure you have some gin on hand in case someone prefers it to vodka.

Once your guests move to the table, we suggest switching over to red wine. While there's nothing wrong with continuing with cocktails through dinner, a nice red wine will pair beautifully with the rich and decadent menu you'll be serving. Almost any red wine will do, but we like to serve either a cabernet sauvignon or a malbec.

SEB SAYS

We recommend decanting older wines (5+ years) 1 hour before your guests arrive, but leave the empty wine bottle and cork next to the decanter in case your guests are interested in seeing which wine you selected.

WINTER WARM-UP

COCKTAILS

ESPRESSO MARTINI (P160)

COSMOPOLITAN (P160)

CLASSIC MARTINI (P161)

CANAPÉS

BAGUETTE WITH:
DUCK RILLETTE (P163)
GARLIC CONFIT (P164)
HERBED CHÈVRE (P164)

GOUGÈRES (P165)

CRANBERRY BAKED BRIE (P166)

FIRST COURSE

HAM + BÉCHAMEL BAKED
TOMATOES (P169)

MAIN COURSE

BOEUF BOURGUIGNON WITH PARISIAN-
STYLE POMMES PURÉE (P170)

CHEESE COURSE (P173)

DESSERT

BAKED STONE FRUIT (P175)

DAME BLANCHE (P175)

PARTY COUNTDOWN:

WINTER WARM-UP

3 THREE DAYS BEFORE

- ○ Send a reminder email or text to your guests with details about the evening.

- ○ Make a grocery and alcohol list.

- ○ Check you have enough plates and glasses for your guests.

- ○ Grocery shop (but leave the cheese shopping for now) and stock up at the liquor store.

- ○ Prepare the duck rillettes and refrigerate in an airtight container.

- ○ Prepare the garlic confit and refrigerate in an airtight container.

2 TWO DAYS BEFORE

- ○ Pick up your garland. When stored correctly between uses in a cool place (or in the fridge), a garland will last for the entire entertaining season.

- ○ Make the pomegranate place cards.

TIME-SAVING TIPS

Instead of serving the cheese course on individual plates, serve it on a large plate in the center of the table.

Lay out all your dinner and glassware the night before so that it's easy to see what you will be serving each course on.

Don't add the cranberry topping to the baked brie—it's equally delicious on its own!

1 THE DAY BEFORE

- ◯ Visit an artisan cheese shop to select the cheeses for your cheese course.
- ◯ Prepare the herbed chèvre and refrigerate in an airtight container.

0 THE DAY OF

- ◯ Start on the beef first thing, since it takes the longest to cook. You can also do this the day before your dinner, because it reheats well.
- ◯ Set the table.
- ◯ Bake the brie.
- ◯ Prepare the ham + béchamel baked tomatoes.
- ◯ Completely prep the baked stone fruit so it's ready for baking at dessert time.
- ◯ Prepare the gougères at the last possible minute—you want them to be eaten warm just as your guests arrive.

ABOVE

COSMOPOLITAN

LEFT

ESPRESSO MARTINI

COCKTAILS

ESPRESSO MARTINI

yield: makes 1 cocktail · prep time: 2 minutes

Ingredients

1⅓ oz vodka
⅔ oz Kahlúa
1 Tbsp + 1 tsp espresso
Espresso beans, for garnish

Method

Place the vodka, Kahlúa, and espresso in a cocktail shaker, add ice, and shake vigorously. Strain into a martini glass and garnish with a few espresso beans. Serve immediately before the foam disappears.

COSMOPOLITAN

yield: makes 1 cocktail · prep time: 2 minutes

Ingredients

1½ oz vodka
2 Tbsp cranberry juice
½ oz Cointreau
1 Tbsp simple syrup, optional (page 11)
Lime wedge or twist, for garnish

Method

Place the vodka, cranberry juice, Cointreau, and simple syrup (if using) in a cocktail shaker, add ice, and shake vigorously. Strain into a martini glass and garnish with a lime wedge or twist.

CLASSIC MARTINI

yield: makes 1 cocktail · prep time: 2 minutes

Ingredients

2½ oz vodka

½ oz dry vermouth

**1 lemon peel twist or 2 olives +
    1 cornichon**

Method

Place the vodka and vermouth in a cocktail shaker,
add ice, and shake vigorously. Strain into a martini
glass and top with either a lemon peel twist or a
skewer with 2 olives and a cornichon.

SHEILA SAYS

*The trick with Cosmopolitans is to only
have one or two. Since they're much
stronger than they taste, having a few
too many can change the course of the
evening for the worse, especially if
you're in charge of cooking!*

SEB SAYS

This recipe takes time, but it's worth it. It keeps for 7-10 days in the fridge, so it's great to make ahead as you move into a week of entertaining.

DUCK RILLETTE

yield: serves 6-8 · prep time: 45 minutes + 2 days in total to chill · cook time: 1½ hours

Ingredients

¼ cup kosher salt

¼ cup packed brown sugar

5 sage leaves

3 thyme sprigs, leaves only

2 rosemary sprigs, leaves only

1 tsp ground white pepper

2 tsp grated lemon zest

5 duck legs (or 1 whole duck)

6 cups chicken stock

2 garlic cloves

4 bay leaves

2 Tbsp Italian parsley,
    finely chopped

2 tsp grated orange zest

Ground allspice

Black pepper

Method

Place the salt, sugar, sage, thyme, rosemary, white pepper, and lemon zest in a small bowl. Mix well to combine.

Pat the duck legs dry with paper towels, then evenly rub the salt-sugar mixture all over it.

Place the duck legs in a bowl or on a baking sheet and let marinate, uncovered, in the fridge for at least 6 hours, or up to overnight.

Remove the duck from the fridge, shake off any excess seasoning, and place in a large stockpot set over high heat. Add enough stock to cover the duck by 1 inch. Add the garlic cloves and bay leaves and bring to a boil.

Once boiling, reduce the heat to a simmer and cook, uncovered, until the duck is fully cooked and tender, about 1½ hours.

Remove from the heat and allow to cool to room temperature. Once at room temperature, put the whole pot in the fridge to chill and let the fat solidify overnight.

The next day, there should be a thick layer of duck fat on the surface. Carefully scrape it off and set aside. You should have at least 1 cup of reserved duck fat.

Reserve ½ cup of the stock, then remove the duck from the pot. Remove and discard the bones and shred the meat.

Place the meat in a medium bowl and mix with 1 Tbsp of the reserved duck fat, ½ cup of the reserved stock, the parsley, orange zest, and a pinch of allspice. Season to taste with black pepper.

Next, pack the duck meat mixture tightly into small, clean glass jars, leaving ½ inch of headspace.

Melt any remaining duck fat in the microwave or in a small pot set over low heat. Pour at least ¼ cup of fat over the duck meat in each jar. The more the better!

Refrigerate until set (overnight at least). Serve in the jar alongside toasted baguette with a small spoon or knife for spreading.

GARLIC CONFIT

yield: serves 6–8 · prep time: 10 minutes +
30 minutes to cool · cook time: 30 minutes

Ingredients

6 garlic bulbs (2 cups of cloves)
3 thyme sprigs
3 bay leaves
1 tsp black peppercorns
¼ tsp pink peppercorns
2 cups olive oil

Method

Peel the garlic cloves. Place them in a small stock-pot, add all the other ingredients, and bring to a simmer over medium heat. Once simmering, reduce the heat to low and cook, uncovered and without stirring, until the garlic is golden and soft, about 30 minutes.

Remove the pot from the heat and, using a slotted spoon, transfer the garlic cloves to a mason jar. Once the oil has cooled, about 30 minutes, pour it over the garlic cloves. Refrigerate until ready to serve. This will keep for up to 2 weeks.

Serve in the jar alongside toasted baguette with a small spoon or knife for spreading. And leftover garlic confit can easily be used to add a punch of flavor to plain pasta or mashed potatoes.

HERBED CHÈVRE

yield: serves 6–8 · prep time: 10 minutes

Ingredients

1 dill sprig, coarsely chopped
1 Tbsp chopped Italian parsley
1 Tbsp thyme leaves
8 oz chèvre log
½ tsp black pepper
½ tsp sweet paprika
½ tsp sea salt
¼ cup olive oil

Method

In a small bowl, mix together the dill, parsley, and thyme.

Using a cheese wire, sharp knife, or unflavored dental floss, cut the chèvre into ¼-inch disks.

Layer the chèvre disks in a glass jar with a pinch each of the mixed fresh herbs, pepper, paprika, and sea salt between each layer. Repeat until the jar is full. Once the jar is full, pour in the oil.

Eat immediately or set aside in the fridge up to overnight. Serve alongside toasted baguette and a small spoon or knife for spreading

GOUGÈRES

yield: makes 12–16 · prep time: 20 minutes · cook time: 25 minutes per batch

Ingredients

½ cup butter
½ cup milk
¼ tsp kosher salt
1 cup all-purpose flour
4 eggs, room temperature
1¼ cups grated gruyère cheese

Method

Preheat the oven to 425°F. Line a baking sheet with parchment paper.

Place the butter, milk, and salt in a medium saucepan, add ½ cup of water, and bring to a boil, without stirring, over medium-high heat.

Once boiling, immediately add the flour and stir constantly with a wooden spoon until the dough pulls away from the sides of the pot and a ball of dough has formed, about 3 minutes.

Transfer the dough to a stand mixer and beat on low speed for 2 minutes or until the outside of the bowl is warm to the touch. Increase the speed to medium-high and add the eggs, one at a time, waiting for each egg to be fully incorporated before adding the next.

Add the gruyère and mix until smooth.

Transfer to a piping bag fitted with a ¾-inch tip (if you don't have one, you can use spoons to make mounds of dough).

Pipe 6 rounds of the dough, each about 1½ inches in diameter, a couple of inches apart onto the prepared baking sheet.

Bake for 10 minutes, then reduce the oven temperature to 350°F and bake until golden, 10–15 minutes.

Remove the gougères from the oven and let them cool for 5 minutes before serving warm. Meanwhile, get the next batch in the oven (remember to start off at 425°F!). Repeat until you've used all the dough.

CRANBERRY BAKED BRIE

yield: serves 6–8 · prep time: 20 minutes · cook time: 25 minutes

Ingredients

1 (16 oz) brie wheel

1 cup pecan halves, lightly toasted

½ cup dry cranberries

½ cup pumpkin seeds, lightly toasted

1½ cups maple syrup

Method

Preheat the oven to 325°F. Line a baking sheet with parchment paper. Place the brie on the prepared baking sheet and bake until soft, 25 minutes.

Meanwhile, in a small pot, warm the pecans, cranberries, pumpkin seeds, and maple syrup over medium heat, mixing until warmed through and the maple syrup evenly coats everything.

Transfer the baked brie to a serving dish just large enough to hold it snugly without crowding and pour the maple syrup mixture overtop. Serve immediately while still hot alongside toasted baguette and a small spoon or knife for spreading.

HAM + BÉCHAMEL BAKED TOMATOES

yield: serves 6 · prep time: 20 minutes · cook time: 20 minutes

Ingredients

6 ripe medium-size beefsteak tomatoes

½ cup butter

½ cup all-purpose flour

2 cups milk

1 cup shredded emmental cheese

1 tsp smooth Dijon mustard

Black pepper

8 oz Black Forest ham, cut into ¼-inch cubes

Method

Preheat the oven to 375°F. Line a baking sheet with parchment paper.

Cut a thin slice from the bottom of each tomato so that it sits flat. Cut the tops off of the tomatoes and set aside.

Hollow out the tomatoes, removing most of the flesh and seeds, but being careful not to scoop out all the flesh and hit the skin. Place the tomatoes on the prepared baking sheet.

Melt the butter in a small saucepan set over medium heat. Whisk in the flour 1 Tbsp at a time until fully incorporated. Slowly add the milk in a steady stream, whisking continuously until the sauce is totally smooth. Cook this béchamel for 2 minutes, still whisking, then stir in the emmental. Add the Dijon and season to taste with pepper. Add all the ham to the béchamel. Stir to combine, then remove from the heat.

Spoon the béchamel-ham filling into the hollowed-out tomatoes and bake until the top of the filling is golden brown and bubbling, about 20 minutes. Serve immediately.

BOEUF BOURGUIGNON WITH PARISIAN-STYLE POMMES PURÉE

yield: serves 6–8 · prep time: 45 minutes · cook time: 2 hours

Ingredients

BOEUF BOURGUIGNON

¼ cup olive oil

12 oz thick-cut bacon, coarsely chopped

1 (4 lb) beef tenderloin, cut in 2-inch pieces and patted dry

1 large yellow onion, finely diced

1 lb carrots, peeled and cut into 2-inch pieces

6 garlic cloves, coarsely chopped, divided

3 Tbsp all-purpose flour

2 cups pearl onions, peeled

5 bay leaves

2 cups red wine

4 cups beef stock

3 Tbsp tomato paste

½ cup salted butter

1 lb cremini mushrooms, stems trimmed and halved

2 Tbsp thyme leaves

¼ cup coarsely chopped Italian parsley

PARISIAN-STYLE POMMES PURÉE

5 large Yukon gold potatoes, peeled and cut into 2-inch pieces

1 cup whipping (36%) cream

½ cup salted butter

3 Tbsp finely chopped garlic

Sea salt and black pepper

Method

FOR THE BOEUF BOURGUIGNON

Heat the oil over medium-high heat in a Dutch oven or a heavy-bottomed pot with a tight-fitting lid. Add the bacon and cook until just crispy, about 10 minutes. Using a slotted spoon, transfer the bacon to a large bowl, leaving the fat in the pot.

Brown the beef in batches on all sides, 2–3 minutes per side. Use the slotted spoon again to transfer the beef to the bowl with the bacon.

Once all the beef has been browned, reduce the heat to medium and add the onions and carrots to the pot (you don't need to wipe it out or clean it first). Cook until the onions are translucent, about 3 minutes. Depending on the size of your pot the leftover oil should be about ¼ inch deep; if there is less, add a little extra oil so that the onions are at least halfway submerged.

Add the bacon, beef, and 3 Tbsp of the garlic to the pot. Sprinkle with the flour and mix well. Cook until all the flour has been absorbed, about 5 minutes.

Add the pearl onions, bay leaves, wine, and enough beef stock to just cover the meat. Stir in the tomato paste.

Bring to a boil, then reduce the heat to low, cover, and simmer until the beef is tender, about 1½ hours.

Once the beef is cooked, heat the butter in a skillet until it just begins to foam. Add the remaining garlic, the mushrooms, and thyme, and stir to combine. Add the mushrooms to the beef, and bring back to a boil. Sprinkle with parsley just before serving.

FOR THE POMMES PURÉE

Place the potatoes in a large stockpot and cover with cold water. Salt the water and bring to a boil over high heat.

Reduce the heat to medium and simmer, uncovered, until the potatoes are fork-tender, about 20 minutes.

Meanwhile, heat the cream, butter, and garlic in a small saucepan over low heat. Set aside once the butter is melted.

Drain the potatoes and transfer them to a stand mixer. Beat them on low speed, slowly adding the cream-butter mixture until incorporated. Increase the speed to high and beat until smooth and fluffy, 3–4 minutes. Season with salt and pepper, to taste. Serve immediately or transfer to an ovenproof dish to keep warm in a 200°F oven.

CHEESE COURSE

yield: serves 6 · prep time: 10 minutes + 1 hour to rest

Ingredients

**9 oz cow's milk cheese
(e.g., brie, emmental,
camembert, bleu, sharp
cheddar)**

**9 oz sheep's milk cheese
(e.g., pecorino, roquefort)**

**9 oz goat's milk cheese
(e.g., chèvre, some varieties
of gouda)**

1½ cups mixed greens

⅛ cup olive oil

¾ Tbsp lemon juice

Sea salt and black pepper

Method

Cut each cheese variety into 6 equal-sized pieces. Arrange the pieces on six serving plates. Keep the cheeses in the fridge until you cut them, as it will make them easier to divide into smaller pieces. Once plated, keep the cheeses at room temperature for 1 hour before serving so they have time to soften.

In a small bowl, combine the mixed greens with the oil, lemon juice, and salt and pepper to taste.

Divide the mixed greens among the plates and serve.

BAKED STONE FRUIT

yield: serves 6–8 · prep time: 20 minutes · cook time: 60-70 minutes

Ingredients

1 Tbsp butter + ¼ cup, divided

2 large bosc pears

3 large apples (McIntosh, empire, and golden delicious all work well)

4 large or 5 small plums

¾ cup packed brown sugar

¼ tsp ground cinnamon

Method

Preheat the oven to 300°F. Grease the bottom and sides of a 7- x 11-inch baking dish with the 1 Tbsp butter.

Core the pears and apples, keeping the skins on, and cut them into ½-inch pieces. If you leave the fruit in larger chunks, you'll have to increase your baking time. Remove the stones from the plums and cut them into ½-inch pieces as well. Place all the cut fruit in the greased baking dish.

Sprinkle the sugar and cinnamon over the fruit. Use your hands to mix the fruit and ensure that everything is well coated.

Cut the remaining ¼ cup butter into small pats and dot the fruit with the butter. Do not toss the fruit.

Bake the fruit until the outer skin darkens and the center of the fruit is soft, carefully tossing every 20 minutes to ensure even cooking, 60–70 minutes. Serve the fruit warm, with a drizzle of the sugar syrup from the baking dish.

DAME BLANCHE

yield: serves 6–8 · prep time: 5 minutes + 15 minutes to cool · cook time: 5 minutes

Ingredients

⅓ cup light corn syrup

⅔ cup cocoa powder

2½ oz dark chocolate, finely chopped

1½ pints vanilla ice cream

Method

Place 1¼ cups of water in a small saucepan over medium-high heat. Add the corn syrup and cocoa powder and bring to a boil, whisking constantly.

Remove from the heat and stir in the chocolate until completely melted.

Allow the chocolate to cool to room temperature, about 15 minutes, and serve over the vanilla ice cream.

SEB SAYS *For a mixed grill dinner, I like to use the grill for every course from the appetizer all the way to the dessert.*

When it comes to enjoying the final days of summer we can't think of anything better than a casual BBQ with friends and family to close out the season. As we bid farewell to summer and say hello to fall, we like to fire up the grill one last time to create the perfect ambience to debate the upcoming NFL season and indulge in one of the last few opportunities of the year to sip cocktails al fresco.

Typically, we recommend including 6 to 8 people for a backyard barbecue, but it's not uncommon for a few last-minute guests to bump those numbers up. For this reason, we like to serve a variety of surf + turf–style dishes to make sure that no matter how many people show up, no one goes hungry.

Backyard barbecues are the perfect opportunity to split up entertaining duties, with one person tending the grill while the other tends to guests and completes any last-minute tasks. Most of the prep for this meal can be done well ahead of time so that you can sit back, relax, and enjoy the nice weather while it lasts.

THE MIXED GRILL

SETTING

Backyard barbecues are all about simplicity, so for this meal we go with less is more and stick to a rustic setting—no fancy tablecloth here. If your backyard permits, nestle the table directly in the grass to really dine in the garden.

Since you're surrounded by the outdoors, you can either use small potted plants for your table décor, or if you're leaning more toward standard florals, use colors that bridge the gap between the table and your garden. We use large mason jars for our florals since they're easy to move around if we need extra room on the table when the food arrives. If you don't have a rustic wooden table, try incorporating rattan chargers into your table setting. They're an inexpensive way to add décor to your table.

TIP

Everyone loves a parting gift. We give each of our guests a customized jar filled with our dry spice rub. Write the name of your guest on top of the jar to give it a personal touch.

SEB SAYS *Consider cooking time as you plan your meal. Salmon, chicken, and sausage will take longer to cook than the steak, so put them on the grill first.*

The evening may begin with a few cocktails as guests arrive but since this meal doesn't feature any canapés or standing appetizers, we choose to seat our guests a bit earlier and serve everything family-style right at the table.

COURSES

The menu at a barbecue is typically full of pretty heavy courses, so we like to start off with two light and fresh appetizers that might not be considered classic barbecue foods.

The first dish we like to bring to the table is a platter of Grilled Bread, Grilled Peaches + Burrata. The peaches and burrata can be plated right before you bring your dish to the table, but rather than toasting the bread in the oven, we like to throw it on the grill for a couple of minutes to give it those beautiful grill marks that guests expect at a backyard barbecue.

For the second appetizer, we suggest a Tomato + Basil Salad, dotted with buffalo mozzarella. Tomatoes are at their prime late in the summer, so we like to use a variety of colors and sizes to bring the best of the season to the table.

Next, it's time to jump into your main course. While we encourage lots of variety at a backyard barbecue, it's important to make sure none of the dishes you serve strays too far from the rest of your menu. So for this meal, we decided to choose meats and seafood that can be combined for our own version of a surf + turf medley.

When choosing seafood for a barbecue we suggest dishes that can be cooked on the grill without too much work. Cedar plank salmon, which requires only a marinade, and butterflied jumbo shrimp, which can be simply cooked with garlic butter, are perfect choices.

For the turf aspect, we like to serve grilled steak, sausage, and marinated chicken. While we always recommend cutting your steak into strips for easy serving, try leaving the T-bone on the platter for the added wow factor as you bring the steak to the table.

To complement your surf + turf, we suggest offering healthy side dishes like corn, grilled Portobello mushroom caps with chèvre, grilled asparagus, and a butter lettuce salad. Aside from the salad, all of these sides can be cooked on the grill, but if you find you're getting a bit short on space, you can prepare and cook them in the kitchen.

While we assume you and your guests will be relatively full at this point in your meal, we still like to offer dessert. One of our favorites is Seb's Famous BBQ Bananas with Ice Cream. It's quick to put together on the grill and a delicious way to end the meal.

WHAT'S ON THE MENU

BEERGARITA

WHAT'S ON THE BAR

The first drink for this party is one of our personal favorites: the Paloma Cocktail. A Paloma is a tequila-based cocktail that features grapefruit juice, lime, and sparkling water or Sprite. Refreshing and delicious, this cocktail is a go-to for us when entertaining because the non-alcoholic version tastes just as good as the original.

Another tequila-based cocktail that goes well with any backyard barbecue is a Beergarita. Our recipe calls for a homemade lime syrup, which might sound daunting but only takes a couple of minutes to prepare and makes all the difference to the finished cocktail.

For non-tequila drinkers, we like to serve a classic Pimm's Punch in a large punch bowl on the bar. Though the choice of garnish is up to you, we recommend sticking to the basics of cucumbers, strawberries, and oranges with a touch of mint to give it a refreshing taste.

THE MIXED GRILL

COCKTAILS

PALOMA COCKTAIL (P188)

PIMM'S PUNCH (P189)

BEERGARITA (P189)

APPETIZERS

GRILLED BREAD, GRILLED PEACHES + BURRATA (P191)

TOMATO + BASIL SALAD WITH BUFFALO MOZZARELLA (P191)

MAIN COURSE

CEDAR PLANK SALMON (P192)

BUTTERFLIED SHRIMP WITH GARLIC BUTTER (P193)

GRILLED STEAK (P196)

GRILLED SAUSAGE (P197)

DRY RUBBED BBQ CHICKEN (P197)

SIDES

PORTOBELLO CAPS WITH CHÈVRE + GOLDEN BREADCRUMBS (P198)

GRILLED ASPARAGUS WITH LEMON (P200)

SIMPLE SALAD WITH RASPBERRY VINAIGRETTE (P200)

FETA + CHILI CORN (P203)

DESSERT

SEB'S FAMOUS BBQ BANANAS WITH ICE CREAM (P204)

PARTY COUNTDOWN:

THE MIXED GRILL

3 THREE DAYS BEFORE

- ○ Send a reminder email or text to your guests with details about the barbecue.

- ○ Make a grocery and alcohol list.

- ○ Ensure you have platters large enough to hold all your surf + turf items, and enough plates and glasses for all your guests.

- ○ Grocery shop, including the spices for the dry rubs, and stock up at the liquor store. Make sure the peaches and tomatoes you choose are super juicy!

2 TWO DAYS BEFORE

- ○ Assemble the dry rubs.

- ○ Cut ribbons and tie them on the vases.

TIME-SAVING TIPS

Offer fewer varieties of meats and seafood. One type of meat and one type of seafood will still be delicious.

Most of these BBQ items can be grilled up to 1 hour ahead of time and kept in the oven on a "Keep Warm" setting (usually 150°F).

Instead of grilling the bananas, make a classic banana split with bananas and ice cream.

Eliminate one of the cocktails and stick with the batched Pimm's punch.

1 THE DAY BEFORE

○ Buy flowers, trim them, and place them in water overnight.

○ Get outside in your backyard and visualize where you will put your table. Does it need to be moved? Is there ample shade?

○ Ensure you have enough propane in your grill! You definitely don't want to run out.

○ Prepare the salad dressing and refrigerate in an airtight container.

0 THE DAY OF

○ Prepare the floral arrangements and set the table.

○ Take out the steak, chicken, and sausage about 30 minutes before grilling to come to room temperature.

○ Prepare the dessert ingredients on a tray (including pre-cut aluminum foil!) so that it's easy to bring out to the grill at dessert time.

○ Grill the peaches and bread.

○ Grill the steak, chicken, and sausage.

○ Grill the salmon and shrimp.

○ Prepare the Pimm's punch.

PALOMA COCKTAIL

COCKTAILS

PALOMA COCKTAIL

yield: makes 1 cocktail · prep time: 5 minutes

Ingredients

1 lime
Coarse sea salt
2 oz tequila
¼ cup grapefruit juice
¼ cup sparkling water, club soda, or Sprite
2 Tbsp lime juice
1 grapefruit wedge, for garnish

Method

Cut the lime in half. Juice one half and cut the other into wedges. Pour a little salt onto a small plate.

Rim a rocks glass by rubbing a lime wedge around the edge and then dipping the rim of the glass in the salt.

Add the tequila, grapefruit juice, sparkling water, and lime juice to the glass and stir gently.

Fill the glass with ice and serve with the grapefruit floating inside.

For a non-alcoholic version, omit the tequila.

TIP

Rimming a glass is a simple way to instantly elevate your cocktail while changing both the flavor and the experience.

PIMM'S PUNCH

yield: makes 6–8 cocktails · prep time: 10 minutes

Ingredients

12 oz Pimm's (about ½ a 750 ml bottle)
3 cups lemon-lime soda (such as Sprite)
1 English cucumber, sliced
1 cup sliced strawberries (about ½ pint)
1 orange, sliced
Mint leaves

Method

Fill a large punch bowl with ice. Add all the ingredients and gently stir.

SEB SAYS

We love Pimm's punch because the recipe is so simple!

BEERGARITA

yield: makes 1 cocktail + 1 cup of simple syrup · prep time: 5 minutes + 1 hour to cool · cook time: 10 minutes

Ingredients

LIME SIMPLE SYRUP
1 cup granulated sugar
10 strips lime zest (about 2 limes)

BEERGARITAS
Coarse salt
¼ cup lime juice (about 2–3 limes)
2 oz tequila
½ oz Grand Marnier
½ oz lime simple syrup
2 oz Corona beer
Lime slices, for garnish

Method

FOR THE SIMPLE SYRUP
In a small saucepan over medium heat, bring 1 cup of water to a boil. Add the sugar and lime zest, stirring until the sugar dissolves. Let cool for about 1 hour, then remove the lime zest. Refrigerate in an airtight container for up to 1 week.

FOR THE BEERGARITAS
Pour some salt onto a small plate. Rim a tall collins glass or pilsner glass by rubbing a lime wedge around the rim and dipping the rim into the salt.

Fill the glass with ice and add the lime juice, tequila, Grand Marnier, and simple syrup. Stir gently. Top with Corona and garnish with the lime.

GRILLED BREAD, GRILLED PEACHES + BURRATA

yield: serves 6–8 · prep time: 30 minutes · cook time: 10 minutes

Ingredients

1 large white baguette
½ cup olive oil
Sea salt and black pepper
5 ripe peaches
1 small burrata ball
2 Tbsp honey
5 mint leaves
½ cup pistachios, lightly salted, optional

Method

Preheat the grill to medium-high.

Slice the baguette into 1-inch-thick slices. Brush with the oil and season lightly with salt and pepper.

Halve and pit the peaches. Brush the cut sides of the peach with the oil.

Grill the bread for about 30 seconds on each side, just until grill marks appear. Set aside on a platter.

Grill the peaches, cut side down, for about 2 minutes. Transfer to the upper rack of the grill, close the lid, and cook until soft and warmed through, about 3 minutes.

Arrange the grilled bread, grilled peaches, and burrata on a large platter. Drizzle them with honey, garnish with mint, and serve with a small bowl of pistachios on the side (if using).

TOMATO + BASIL SALAD WITH BUFFALO MOZZARELLA

yield: serves 6–8 · prep time: 15 minutes

Ingredients

3 large ripe heirloom tomatoes
1 pint heirloom cherry tomatoes
6–8 medium bocconcini balls
¼ cup olive oil
Sea salt and black pepper
1 bunch basil

Method

Cut the heirloom tomatoes into wedges and the cherry tomatoes in half.

Arrange the tomatoes on a large platter with the bocconcini. Drizzle the oil over the entire platter and season with salt and pepper. Scatter the basil leaves overtop.

SEB SAYS

We like to use heirloom tomatoes because they come in such beautiful colors. If heirlooms aren't available, you can use very ripe vine tomatoes.

CEDAR PLANK SALMON

yield: serves 6–8 · prep time: 15 minutes + 2 hours–overnight to soak · cook time: 30 minutes

Ingredients

2 (each 9½- x 7½- x ¼-inch) cedar planks

6 Tbsp smooth Dijon mustard

5 Tbsp packed brown sugar or maple syrup

8 (each 6 oz) salmon fillets

Sea salt and black pepper

Method

Soak the cedar planks in water for at least 2 hours, or up to overnight.

Preheat the grill to medium-high.

In a small bowl, mix together the Dijon and sugar. Set aside.

Drain off any excess water from the cedar planks. Lay 4 salmon fillets on each cedar plank, making sure they are evenly spaced.

Spread the mustard mixture over the top and sides of each fillet. Season with salt and pepper.

Place the cedar planks in the center of the hot grill grate, away from the direct flame. Close the lid and cook until the internal temperature reads 135°F on a meat thermometer, 25–30 minutes. If you're using a thicker cedar plank, the cooking will take longer.

Remove the plank from the grill and serve the salmon immediately, using the cedar plank as the platter.

TIP

Keep a mister bottle filled with water by the barbecue just in case the edges of the cedar plank start to burn.

BUTTERFLIED SHRIMP WITH GARLIC BUTTER

yield: serves 6–8 · prep time: 20 minutes · cook time: 10 minutes

Ingredients

1 cup butter

¼ cup chopped Italian parsley

1 Tbsp minced garlic

2 lb shrimp (6/8 count), shell on and deveined

¼ cup olive oil

Sea salt and black pepper

2 lemons, cut into wedges

Method

In a medium bowl, mix together the butter, parsley, and garlic until smooth and well incorporated.

Using a sharp paring knife, butterfly the shrimp by carefully slicing them along the length of their backs (where it has been deveined), making sure not to cut all the way through. Gently press the shrimp flat and set aside.

Preheat your grill to medium-high.

Brush the shrimp with the oil and grill, cut side down, for about 3 minutes. Flip the shrimp and grill until the flesh turns white and opaque, about 3 minutes.

Transfer the grilled shrimp to a platter and place about 1 tsp of the garlic butter mixture on top of each one while still hot so that the butter melts.

Season to taste with salt and pepper and serve with lemon wedges on the side.

LEFT

CLOCKWISE:
GRILLED
SAUSAGE, DRY
RUBBED BBQ
CHICKEN, GRILLED
STEAK

TOP

BUTTERFLIED
SHRIMP WITH
GARLIC

BOTTOM

CEDAR PLANK
SALMON

GRILLED STEAK

yield: serves 6–8 · prep time: 5 minutes + 40 minutes to rest · cook time: 20 minutes

Ingredients

1 (2 lb) cote de boeuf, about 2½ inches thick

¼ cup olive oil

2 Tbsp coarse sea salt

2 Tbsp rosemary leaves

½ tsp chili flakes, optional

Black pepper

Method

Remove the steak from the fridge at least 30 minutes before grilling to allow it to come to room temperature.

Preheat the grill to high. Preheat the oven to 375°F. Line a baking sheet with parchment paper.

Brush the entire steak with the oil.

Grill the steak on each side until dark grill marks form, about 5 minutes per side.

Transfer the steak to the prepared baking sheet and cook it in the oven until the internal temperature reaches 130°F, 7–10 minutes. Keep a close eye on it as ovens vary and you don't want to overcook the meat. Remove the steak from the oven, tent loosely with foil, and allow to rest for at least 10 minutes.

Slice the meat into ½-inch-thick slices along the bone to remove the meat completely. Transfer to a serving platter and arrange the meat slices along the bone for presentation. Season generously with the salt, rosemary, chili flakes (if using), and pepper to taste.

SHEILA SAYS

Starting your steak on the grill and finishing it in the oven frees up grill space and makes entertaining easier.

GRILLED SAUSAGE

yield: serves 6–8 · prep time: 5 minutes + 5 minutes to rest · cook time: 15 minutes

Ingredients

6 sausages (pork sausages such as Italian, chorizo, kielbasa, or andouille all work well)

Method

Preheat the grill to high.

Pierce the sausages a few times with the tip of a sharp knife to ensure even cooking and avoid cracking or bursting. Grill the sausages, turning halfway through cooking, until their internal temperature reaches 160°F, about 15 minutes in total.

Remove from the grill and let rest for 5 minutes before slicing. Using a few different types of sausages and slicing them up allows your guests to try a little bit of everything.

DRY RUBBED BBQ CHICKEN

yield: serves 6–8 · prep time: 15 minutes + 2 hours–overnight to marinate · cook time: 45 minutes

Ingredients

2 Tbsp chili powder
2 Tbsp garlic powder
2 Tbsp black pepper
2 Tbsp dry mustard powder
2 Tbsp onion powder
2 Tbsp sweet paprika
2 tsp dry basil
2 tsp dry oregano
2 tsp dry tarragon
2 tsp dry thyme
2 tsp fennel seeds
½ tsp cayenne pepper, optional
1 (2½ lb) whole chicken or 6–7 bone-in, skin-on chicken breasts

Method

In a small bowl, whisk all the spices together until fully combined. Rub the chicken liberally with the spice rub and refrigerate for at least 2 hours, or up to overnight.

Preheat the grill to high.

Grill the chicken until the internal temperature reaches 165°F and the juices run clear, about 45 minutes to 1 hour. Sometimes we like to turn or flip the chicken depending on the hot spots of the barbecue. You can either keep the chicken whole and carve it after cooking or cut the thighs, legs, and breasts off beforehand to speed up the cooking time.

Serve on a large platter.

Note

We like to double the amount of rub and then package it up in 4 oz mason jars for our guests to take home. Write instructions on a small note card for your guests: Rub 2 chicken breasts liberally with the spice rub and marinate in the fridge for 2 hours or up to overnight. Grill the chicken over high heat until the internal temperature reaches 165°F and the juices run clear.

PORTOBELLO CAPS WITH CHÈVRE + GOLDEN BREADCRUMBS

yield: serves 6–8 · prep time: 20 minutes + 10 minutes to marinate · cook time: 15 minutes

Ingredients

GOLDEN BREADCRUMB TOPPING

3 Tbsp olive oil

½ cup panko breadcrumbs

1 Tbsp thyme leaves

1 Tbsp finely chopped Italian parsley

1 Tbsp finely chopped rosemary leaves

1 tsp sea salt

½ tsp black pepper

MUSHROOMS

8 Portobello mushrooms

6 Tbsp olive oil

2 garlic cloves, minced

2 Tbsp thyme leaves

Sea salt and black pepper

8 oz chèvre

Method

FOR THE BREADCRUMB TOPPING

In a small bowl, mix the oil with the panko, thyme, parsley, rosemary, salt, and pepper until all the ingredients are well combined and the mixture resembles wet sand.

Place the breadcrumb mixture in a dry, medium skillet over medium heat. Toast the breadcrumbs, stirring constantly. Keep a close eye on them as they can go from toasted to burnt in seconds.

Remove the breadcrumbs from the pan and spread them over a large plate to cool.

FOR THE MUSHROOMS

Gently remove any dirt from the mushrooms with damp paper towel. Remove and discard the stem by snapping it at its base.

In a small bowl, mix together the oil, garlic, thyme, and salt and pepper to taste. Brush this mixture all over each Portobello cap and set aside for at least 10 minutes to marinate.

Heat the grill to medium-high. Grill the Portobellos, gill side down, until dark grill marks appear, about 5 minutes.

Flip the caps and dot with the chèvre. Grill until the chèvre has softened, about 7 minutes. If the mushrooms are starting to burn, transfer them to the upper rack of the grill to let the chèvre continue to melt.

Remove the Portobellos from the grill and use a spoon to smooth out the chèvre if required. Top each one with golden breadcrumbs and serve.

GRILLED ASPARAGUS WITH LEMON

yield: serves 6–8 · prep time: 10 minutes · cook time: 5 minutes

Ingredients
2 lb asparagus
¼ cup olive oil
Sea salt and black pepper
2 Tbsp grated lemon zest

Method
Wash the asparagus. Snap off and discard the tough ends. Place in a large bowl with the oil, season to taste with salt and pepper, and toss until all the asparagus is evenly coated.

Preheat the grill to medium-high.

Place the asparagus perpendicular to the direction of the grill grates. Cook until softened and charred, about 5 minutes.

Transfer to a serving platter, and top with a sprinkle of lemon zest.

SIMPLE SALAD WITH RASPBERRY VINAIGRETTE

yield: serves 6–8 · prep time: 15 minutes

Ingredients
RASPBERRY VINAIGRETTE
1 cup raspberries + extra for salad garnish
¼ cup rice wine vinegar
¼ cup cold water
1 Tbsp honey
¼ tsp sea salt
¼ tsp black pepper
¾ cup olive oil

SALAD
1 ripe avocado
1 (14 oz) can hearts of palm, rinsed and drained
8 cups mixed greens
1 small red onion, thinly sliced
Sea salt and black pepper

Method
FOR THE VINAIGRETTE
Place all the ingredients except the oil in a blender. Process on medium speed until completely smooth. Gradually increase the speed while you slowly add the oil in a steady stream until emulsified. Refrigerate in an airtight container for up to 3 days.

FOR THE SALAD
Slice the avocado in half and remove the pit. Peel the avocados and cut them lengthwise into thin slices.

Slice the hearts of palm into ½-inch rounds.

Arrange the mixed greens, avocado, red onion, and hearts of palm (in that order) on a serving platter. Sprinkle a few raspberries overtop. Season to taste with salt and pepper and drizzle with vinaigrette right before serving.

FETA + CHILI CORN

yield: serves 6–8 · prep time: 15 minutes + 10 minutes to chill · cook time: 30 minutes

Ingredients

6 corn cobs

¼ cup olive oil

Sea salt and black pepper

6 Tbsp butter, melted

6 oz crumbled feta

3 garlic cloves, minced

2 tsp chili powder

1 cup cilantro, coarsely chopped

2 limes, cut into wedges

Method

Fill a large stockpot two-thirds full with salted water and bring to a boil over high heat. Prepare an ice bath.

Peel the corn and trim off the ends.

Boil the corn for 12 minutes, then immediately transfer to the ice bath for 10 minutes to stop the cooking process. Break each cob in half so you end up with 12 cobs.

Preheat the grill to medium-high. Brush each corn cob with the oil and season lightly with salt and pepper.

Grill until grill marks appear, rotating as needed, about 15 minutes total. Remove from the grill and place on a serving platter.

Drizzle the melted butter over the corn and garnish each cob with feta, garlic, chili powder, and cilantro. Serve with lime wedges on the side.

SEB'S FAMOUS BBQ
BANANAS WITH ICE CREAM

yield: serves 6 · prep time: 10 minutes · cook time: 10 minutes

Ingredients

6 ripe bananas
6 tsp brown sugar
1½ tsp vanilla extract
1 pint vanilla ice cream, for serving

Method

Preheat the barbecue to high.

Using a paring knife, slice along the skin of each banana.
Stop 1 inch from the stem and be sure to cut through only the
skin, not the flesh. Gently pull back the skins of the banana
to create a "boat."

Cover the grill with a piece of aluminum foil about 12 inches
long.

Place the bananas on the foil, close the lid of the barbecue,
and cook until the bananas have slightly softened, about
3 minutes.

Open the lid and sprinkle ½ tsp of sugar and ⅛ tsp of vanilla
evenly inside the cut of each banana. Close the lid and cook
for 2 minutes.

Open the lid, add another ½ tsp of sugar and ⅛ tsp of vanilla
to each banana, and cook with the lid closed until the interior
of the bananas has softened, about 2 minutes.

Remove the bananas from the grill and serve warm with
vanilla ice cream.

When you think of outdoor summer dining, what's the first thing that comes to mind? Many people have great memories of celebrating the warm weather and entertaining outdoors, and we're no different. While we're always eager to welcome the start of summer, in our books it doesn't officially start until we are able to entertain in the traditional southern French style with a Mediterranean lunch.

In the south of France, the main attraction of any Mediterranean lunch is the farm-to-table aspect of the meal. Before you begin preparing Grilled Loup de Mer (European sea bass), Deconstructed Niçoise Salad, or extravagant crudités baskets, recognize that it's important to use ingredients that are as fresh as possible and grown as close as possible to home. Not only will this help accentuate the flavors, but it will also allow guests to enjoy the natural colors and smells of fresh produce—just as they would at some of the iconic restaurants along Pampelonne Beach in Saint Tropez.

While this menu can be enjoyed as lunch or dinner, we like to combine the two with "linner," and let the meal move slowly and indulgently. Our favorite thing about a casual Mediterranean lunch is that while it may begin as early as 1:00 pm or as late as 3:00 pm, oftentimes we find ourselves still drinking, dining, and laughing around the table into the early (or sometimes late) hours of the evening. Because of the laid-back aspect of this meal, we use it as an opportunity to invite some of our dearest friends and family to join us in celebrating summer, including our good friends, the Doerges, who introduced us to the term linner!

In our family, it goes without saying that no Mediterranean or Saint Tropez–style lunch would be complete without rosé! Though we drink rosé simply on ice, over the years we've been introduced to a few rosé-based cocktails that are definitely worth trying.

SEB SAYS *It wouldn't be a Mediterranean lunch without my favorite French mayonnaise—Lesieur, la classique! Keep a few small bowls scattered across your table for guests to enjoy with their fish, baguette, or hard-boiled eggs.*

SETTING

When you're planning a lunch like this one, creating the right look is often the most important part of the table setting. It will absolutely set the tone for the entire event. Before you take out your favorite plateware, do a quick search to see if you have anything that would tie in nicely with a Provençal theme. Décor from the south of France is eclectic with lots of different patterns, textures, and colors, so don't be afraid to mix and match your serving pieces.

Start by covering your table with a long table runner, if possible, in a light pastel color, before adding simple plates and cutlery. Some people combine their runner with a more elaborate combination of tablewares, but we often find that basic flatware will do as the runner itself is quite bold. Sticking with the theme of simplicity, a clear wine and water glass at each place setting is usually all that's needed in terms of glassware. Sometimes we set three glasses or more depending on what wines are being served, but in this case we're sticking to rosé only, so a single wine glass will do.

Smaller bouquet arrangements of artichokes, lemons, and lavender spread across the table are an easy way to evoke the Mediterranean seaside.

We also like to incorporate a large centerpiece of fresh crudités on our table. It's a fun way to add color to the table, but because fresh crudités are also a staple at many of Saint Tropez's most famous beach clubs, it also serves as an authentic first course for the meal.

Since you'll likely be hosting your guests outside, make sure you prepare for the elements. We like to set up a few umbrellas or awnings to create shade and keep our guests cool throughout lunch. If you want to go one step further, or you're anticipating a hotter than normal day, try placing a personal paddle fan at each place setting. Placing cushions on the back of each chair is another great way to help keep your guests comfortable.

TIP

Nothing ruins an outdoor meal quite like bugs. In order to set yourself up for success, place bug traps away from your table before your guests arrive. This should help keep mosquitos and other unwanted critters away from the table for the duration of your meal.

WHAT'S ON THE MENU

The first thing you need to remember when it comes to our menu for this lunch is that it may seem like there is too much variety, but that is entirely the point. Imagine a big table made up of friends and family, all of them passing large dishes around and serving themselves their favorite courses. Not everyone may indulge in each dish but a family-style platter meal allows everyone to pick more of the items they like while avoiding the items they are less fond of. You can, of course, pick and choose the courses you want to use for your lunch. Entertaining is all about finding inspiration and adapting the ideas to your own skill or comfort level.

In lieu of traditional canapés, we kick off our Mediterranean lunch with the perfect shared platter: Crudités with Anchovy Dipping Sauce, the crudité basket that doubles as our centerpiece. Though you can't make a wrong choice when deciding what vegetables to include, we like to feature a mix of field carrots, tomatoes, cucumbers, fennel, cauliflower, and mini radishes. Use whole vegetables with the stems still on for that fresh-from-the-farm feel. We also like to serve hard-boiled eggs on a separate plate, as it's a staple of any southern French lunch.

As your guests nibble on the selection of crudités, it's time to bring your Deconstructed Niçoise Salad to the table. Since the ingredients in this dish can be similar to the crudités, it's important to make sure you include new vegetables like beets, mini potatoes, and romaine hearts for some variety. The dressing should be served in a smaller bowl off to the side for guests to help themselves.

We follow these with two more classic European summer dishes: Prosciutto + Melon Florets and Steamed Whole Artichokes with Dipping Sauce. Quick and easy to prepare, prosciutto and melon are a staple in restaurants all along the Mediterranean. There are many ways to present them together. You may be most familiar with a slice of prosciutto wrapped around a wedge of melon, but we love the elegant look of ultra-thinly sliced prosciutto and shaved melon ribbons presented in small bunches or florets on a platter.

The artichokes need between 45 and 60 minutes to steam, so it's important to manage your time well to have them ready to serve before the main course. You can prepare the dipping sauce a few minutes before the artichokes are ready. Once both elements of this appetizer are ready, bring them to the table on a platter and serve alongside the melon and prosciutto dish.

Next, it's time for the most exciting part of your Mediterranean lunch: the fresh fish! Although any whole white fish will work well, if you have the opportunity to get a whole Loup de Mer (European sea bass), branzino, or sea

TIP

Compound butter can be made months in advance and stored in the fridge or freezer. Use it to flavor rice, chicken, fish, or potatoes, or spread it on a warm baguette.

IMAGE OPPOSITE

GRILLED LOUP DE MER AND RICE WITH COMPOUND BUTTER

bream from your local fish market, we would highly recommend trying them. If none of these are available, ask your fishmonger for a white fish alternative, but make sure you tell them whether you're planning to grill the fish on the barbecue or bake it in the oven, as that will affect how the fishmonger prepares it. For grilling, you want the scales left on so the fish stays together when you flip it; for baking, the fish can be descaled.

One of our favorite dishes to pair alongside this fish is Rice with Compound Butter. It's a beautiful accent for the Loup de Mer and doesn't overpower the flavors of the fish. Whether you follow our recipe, or adjust it to make your own, compound butter is an easy way to upgrade standard butter with lots of added flavor.

After a meal with so many courses, we like to finish with a simple Fruit Tart. We use peaches and apricots in the recipe we've shared here, but blueberries, blackberries, and strawberries are all great options. This classic dessert can be topped with vanilla ice cream or crème fraîche.

WHAT'S ON THE BAR

For our Mediterranean lunch we like to offer beverages that are a bit lighter and brighter than we would typically serve at lunch or dinner. That's why both of the drinks we've included in this chapter revolve around rosé! Whether it's mixed into a cocktail or served on ice, rosé is one of the most versatile summer wines.

The first rosé-based cocktail we like to serve is Rosé Sangria. Instead of using traditional fruits like apples or oranges, try experimenting with grapefruits, raspberries, and nectarines to create a delicious cocktail while keeping the color of your rosé intact.

For those who are looking for a slightly stronger cocktail, we are offering the Rosé Floater. Since more than just a few ingredients are needed for this drink, consider serving it as a batched cocktail so you don't spend your entire afternoon mixing drinks in the kitchen.

Finally, make sure to have a few bottles of rosé on hand for those who prefer drinking it plain on ice. Different types of rosé can differ in taste as much as different white or red wines, so it's important to have variety among your selection. Keep each bottle on ice for the duration of your lunch, but also be sure to have a separate bucket of clean ice nearby for your guests to add to their drinks.

A MEDITERRANEAN LUNCH

COCKTAILS

ROSÉ SANGRIA (P217)

ROSÉ FLOATER (P217)

CANAPÉS

CRUDITÉS WITH ANCHOVY DIPPING
SAUCE (ANCHOIADE) (P218)

DECONSTRUCTED NIÇOISE SALAD WITH
CLASSIC AIOLI + LEMON VINAIGRETTE
(P221)

PROSCIUTTO + MELON FLORETS (P222)

STEAMED WHOLE ARTICHOKES WITH
DIPPING SAUCE (P222)

MAIN COURSE

GRILLED LOUP DE MER (P224)

RICE WITH COMPOUND BUTTER (P225)

DESSERT

FRUIT TART (P226)

PARTY COUNTDOWN:

A MEDITERRANEAN LUNCH

3 THREE DAYS BEFORE

○ Send a reminder email or text to your guests with details about the lunch.

○ Find fans and a table runner. This is a more elevated lunch than the meals you've seen so far in this book, so you want to be sure ahead of time that you have the pieces you need to properly convey your theme and create the right feel at the table.

○ Make your grocery and alcohol lists.

○ Make sure you have enough plates and glasses for your guests.

2 TWO DAYS BEFORE

○ Grocery shop (but leave the lavender and fish for now) and buy the alcohol.

○ Make the compound butter and refrigerate in an airtight container.

○ Make the fan place cards.

TIME- SAVING TIPS

Since this meal is served as a lunch, you will have less time to prepare on the actual day. We recommend having most things done the night before to create a stress-free morning that will set you up for an enjoyable afternoon.

If you want to set the table the day before, either turn your glasses and plates upside down so you can simply turn them over before your guests arrive, or use a second tablecloth to completely cover the table overnight.

Reduce your menu by skipping the prosciutto and melon course and serving the steamed artichokes alongside the fish and rice.

While we like serving the artichokes warm, to save time you can steam them the night before and serve them chilled with the same sauce or with a warmed-up beurre blanc sauce.

1 — THE DAY BEFORE

◯ Buy fresh or dried lavender. If you buy fresh, store it in a cool room or basement.

◯ Set aside the plates, serving platters, and cutlery you will be using. This will save you time the next morning.

◯ Make the Dijon, lemon vinaigrette, aioli, and anchovy sauces and refrigerate in airtight containers.

◯ Wash all the vegetables for the crudités and refrigerate in airtight containers.

◯ Purchase the fish, wrap it well, and refrigerate.

0 — THE DAY OF

◯ Set the table.

◯ Prepare and bake the fruit tart.

◯ Assemble the crudités platter.

◯ Assemble the salad and refrigerate.

◯ Steam the artichokes.

◯ Prepare the prosciutto and melon right before you're ready to serve them.

TOP

ROSÉ SANGRIA

BOTTOM

ROSÉ FLOATER

ROSÉ SANGRIA

yield: makes 6–8 cocktails · prep time: 15 minutes

Ingredients

1 (750 ml) bottle rosé, chilled

¼ cup (60 ml) triple sec, Grand Marnier,
    or Cointreau

1 oz brandy

2 peaches or nectarines, sliced

1 blood orange, skin on, sliced into rounds

1 pink grapefruit, skin on, sliced into rounds

1 pint raspberries

1 cup chilled sparkling water + more for serving

Method

Place all the ingredients in a large pitcher and stir
gently. Serve in short rocks glasses with ice and top
with additional sparkling water.

SHEILA SAYS

*Freeze the fruit and use them
as ice cubes to help keep the
Rosé Sangria cold for longer.*

ROSÉ FLOATER

yield: makes 1 cocktail · prep time: 10 minutes

Ingredients

2 oz vodka

¾ oz St. Germain elderflower liqueur

1½ Tbsp lemon juice

½ oz cognac or peach or apricot brandy

1 oz rosé wine

Edible flower, for garnish

Method

Place the vodka, elderflower liqueur, lemon juice,
and cognac in a cocktail shaker. Add ice and shake
vigorously for 10–15 seconds. Strain into a goblet or
stemless wine glass filled with ice. Top with the rosé
and garnish with an edible flower.

CRUDITÉS WITH ANCHOVY DIPPING SAUCE (ANCHOIADE)

yield: serves 6–8 · prep time: 30 minutes · cook time: 10 minutes

Ingredients

CRUDITÉS

6 eggs

1 bunch field carrots (6–8)

2 cauliflowers

3 ripe heirloom tomatoes

1 bunch red radishes

1 English cucumber

2 red bell peppers

1 head celery

1 bulb fennel

1 bunch basil, optional

ANCHOVY DIPPING SAUCE (ANCHOIADE)

8 anchovy fillets packed in oil

2 garlic cloves

½ cup brick-style cream cheese

½ cup lemon juice (3–4 lemons)

½ cup olive oil

1 Tbsp smooth Dijon mustard

1 Tbsp capers

Black pepper

Method

FOR THE CRUDITÉS

Bring a large pot of water to a boil over high heat and prepare an ice bath. Add the eggs, reduce the heat, and simmer until the eggs are hard-boiled, about 10 minutes. Transfer the eggs to the ice bath to stop the cooking process and set aside to cool.

For this crudités platter, you want to offer both whole and cut vegetables to make it easy for guests to choose only as much as they want.

Peel the carrots and trim the stems to 1-inch long. Leave 1 cauliflower whole, and break the other into large florets. Leave 2 heirloom tomatoes whole, and cut the other into quarters.

Wash the radishes well to remove any dirt. Leave them all whole, but trim the stems to 1-inch long.

Cut the cucumber in half horizontally. Cut one half lengthwise, then cut each length into halves or thirds crosswise to make cucumber sticks. These will be served alongside the half cucumber to give guests the option to grab cucumber sticks, or cut their own serving.

Cut the bell peppers in half lengthwise, removing the core and seeds, or leave whole. Gently separate the inner and outer ribs of the celery, and cut a few of them in half, leaving the rest whole.

Remove the green stalks from the fennel, peel and discard the outer layer, and cut the inner bulb into quarters. Remove and discard the fibrous inner core.

Arrange the whole and cut vegetables on a large serving platter then insert the bunch of basil (if using) in between the whole vegetables for garnish. Serve chilled or at room temperature with the hard-boiled eggs and anchovy dipping sauce on a side plate. Have a few sharp knives within reach for guests to cut their own servings from the whole vegetables.

FOR THE SAUCE

Place all the ingredients in a blender or food processor and purée until smooth. Refrigerate in an airtight container for up to 1 week. Transfer to small bowls to serve with the crudités.

DECONSTRUCTED NIÇOISE SALAD WITH CLASSIC AIOLI + LEMON VINAIGRETTE

yield: serves 6–8 · prep time: 15 minutes + 5 minutes to rest · cook time: 30 minutes

Ingredients

DECONSTRUCTED NIÇOISE SALAD

½ lb green beans

1 lb miniature white or
    red potatoes

4 eggs

1 lb ahi tuna

Olive oil

1 bunch field carrots (6–8 carrots)

3 romaine hearts

1 bunch red radishes

1 cup Kalamata olives

CLASSIC AIOLI

3 large egg yolks

2 garlic cloves, minced

2 Tbsp lemon juice

½ tsp smooth Dijon mustard

⅓ cup canola oil

2 tsp ice water

⅓ cup olive oil

Sea salt

LEMON VINAIGRETTE

⅓ cup lemon juice (about
    2 lemons)

⅔ cup olive oil

Sea salt and black pepper

Method

FOR THE SALAD

Bring a large pot of water to a boil over high heat. Prepare an ice bath.

Cook the beans in the boiling water until they turn a vibrant green color, 1–2 minutes. Transfer immediately to the ice bath to stop the cooking process.

Bring the water back to a boil and cook the potatoes until cooked but still slightly firm, about 10 minutes. Set aside to cool.

Bring the water back to a boil again, add the eggs, and cook until hard-boiled, about 10 minutes. Transfer to the ice bath to stop the cooking process. Once they're cool enough to handle, peel and halve them.

Heat a medium skillet over medium-high heat until very hot. Pat dry the tuna, drizzle lightly with the oil, and gently place it in the hot pan. Cook until the outer skin is an opaque white, about 3 minutes on each side. Be careful not to overcook, as we want the inside of the tuna to be bright pink. Remove from the pan and rest for at least 5 minutes before cutting into cubes. Set aside to cool.

Peel the carrots and trim the stems to 1-inch long.

Quarter the hearts of romaine lettuce, keeping the cores intact. Drizzle them with the lemon vinaigrette if serving within 1 hour. Otherwise, drizzle just before serving.

Wash the radishes well, trim the stems to 1-inch long, and cut them in half.

Arrange the beans, potatoes, eggs, tuna, carrots, dressed romaine, radishes, and olives on a large platter. Serve with the aioli on the side.

FOR THE AIOLI

In a large bowl, whisk together the egg yolks, garlic, lemon juice, and Dijon until fully combined.

Whisking continuously, slowly pour in the canola oil in a steady stream. Add the ice water and whisk until fully combined.

Still whisking, add the olive oil in a slow, steady stream. Season to taste with salt. Refrigerate in an airtight container until ready to serve.

FOR THE VINAIGRETTE

Whisk together the lemon juice and oil in a small bowl until emulsified, then immediately pour over the lettuce before the dressing separates. If making the vinaigrette ahead, it may separate after some time in the fridge—let it come to room temperature, and whisk again. Season to taste with salt and pepper.

PROSCIUTTO + MELON FLORETS

yield: serves 6–8 · prep time: 20 minutes

Ingredients
2 large cantaloupes
24 slices of thinly sliced prosciutto

Method
Cut the cantaloupe in half, peel the skin, and remove the seeds. Cut each half in half again. Shave each piece into long thin slices using a mandolin or a vegetable peeler.

On a large serving platter, make piles of prosciutto, about 3 pieces per mound. Pinch together a small bunch of cantaloupe ribbons and place them on top of the prosciutto, creating florets. Serve immediately.

STEAMED WHOLE ARTICHOKES WITH DIPPING SAUCE

yield: serves 6–8 · prep time: 15 minutes · cook time: 45 minutes

Ingredients
4 large artichokes
1 cup mayonnaise
2 Tbsp lemon juice
1 Tbsp smooth Dijon mustard
1 tsp granulated sugar
1 tsp garlic powder

Method
Fill a large pot fitted with a steamer basket and a tight-fitting lid with generously salted water and bring to a simmer over medium-high heat.

Prepare the artichokes by cutting 1 inch off the tops so that the leaves have a straight edge to stand on.

Place the artichokes in the steamer basket, cut side down, cover, and steam until tender, about 45 minutes. You'll know they're ready when you can easily pluck out a leaf.

Make the dipping sauce by placing the mayonnaise, lemon juice, Dijon, sugar, and garlic powder in a blender and blending on high speed until smooth. Season to taste with sea salt. Serve the dipping sauce alongside the steamed artichokes. The dipping sauce is best eaten as soon as it's made.

TIP

While ideally you would serve your artichokes warm, they hold their temperature well and are equally delicious lukewarm or at room temperature, so don't stress too much about getting them to the table hot.

GRILLED LOUP DE MER

yield: serves 6–8 · prep time: 10 minutes · cook time: 25 minutes

Ingredients

5 lemons, divided

4 (each 2 lb) whole sea bass (or similar round fish), gutted

1 bunch sage leaves

1 bunch Italian parsley

Sea salt and black pepper

Olive oil, for drizzling

Method

Preheat the barbecue to medium-high.

Slice 3 of the lemons into rounds, approximately ⅛-inch thick.

Fill the cavity of each fish with 1 sprig of sage, 1 sprig of parsley, and 3 lemon rounds. Season to taste with salt and pepper, then gently close each fish and secure with kitchen twine.

Drizzle each fish evenly with oil. Grill just long enough to create grill marks on the skin, about 2 minutes on each side.

Carefully place each fish on the upper rack of the barbecue.

Cook until the internal temperature of the fish reaches 140°F at the thickest part. Depending on the size of fish and strength of your barbecue, this could take anywhere from 20 to 25 minutes.

Cut the remaining 2 lemons into wedges.

Remove the fish from the grill, cut the twine, and serve on a platter with the lemon wedges, remaining whole sage and parsley leaves, and a final drizzle of oil.

RICE WITH COMPOUND BUTTER

yield: serves 6–8 + makes 2 cups of butter · prep time: 20 minutes + 4 hours–overnight · cook time: 15 minutes

Ingredients

COMPOUND BUTTER

2 cups salted butter, softened

¼ cup finely chopped flat-leaf parsley

1 Tbsp finely chopped sage

1 Tbsp finely chopped chives

2 Tbsp grated orange zest

1 garlic clove, minced

½ tsp sea salt

¼ tsp black pepper

RICE

3 cups jasmine rice

Method

FOR THE BUTTER

In a medium bowl, mix together the butter, parsley, sage, chives, and orange zest. Add the garlic, salt, and pepper. Mix together until everything is evenly distributed.

Place a 15- x 15-inch sheet of parchment paper on the counter in front of you and spoon the compound butter onto it in the shape of a log. Use the parchment paper to help roll the compound butter into a tight log about 1½ inches in diameter, twisting the ends to close.

Wrap the parchment-wrapped log in plastic wrap to ensure a good seal and place in the fridge or freezer for at least 4 hours, but preferably overnight, until ready to serve.

FOR THE RICE

Remove the compound butter from the fridge and cut 6 thin slices. Each slice should measure about ¼-inch thick. You will have lots of leftover compound butter that, when frozen, will last for months so you can just remove the log from the freezer, slice off what you need, re-wrap, and return to the freezer. Another great use for compound butter is on grilled steak.

Bring 6 cups of water to a boil in a large pot over medium-high heat.

Once the water is boiling, cook the rice until the water has been absorbed, about 15 minutes. Remove from the heat, let the rice rest for about 5 minutes, then fluff with a fork.

Mix 4 slices of the compound butter into the warm rice, ensuring every grain of rice is shiny and coated with butter.

Serve the warm rice on a large platter, topped with the remaining 2 slices of compound butter.

FRUIT TART

yield: serves 6–8 · prep time: 30 minutes + 10 minutes to cool · cook time: 50 minutes

Ingredients

FRANGIPANE

½ cup butter

½ cup granulated sugar

3 eggs, divided

1 cup almond flour, divided

1 Tbsp all-purpose flour

1 tsp vanilla extract

½ tsp grated lemon zest

CRUST

1 (9-inch) frozen par-baked pie crust, thawed according to package directions

FILLING

2 cups thinly sliced stone fruit (pears, apricots, etc.)

¼ cup granulated sugar

½ cup melted butter

¼ cup crushed pistachios

Icing sugar, for serving

1 cup crème fraîche, optional

Method

FOR THE FRANGIPANE

In a stand mixer fitted with the paddle attachment, beat the butter and sugar on high speed until light and fluffy, about 4 minutes.

Reduce the mixer speed to low. With the mixer running, add 1 egg and ⅓ cup of the almond flour. Mix until fully combined. Repeat twice until the eggs and all the almond flour are incorporated, scraping down the sides of the bowl between additions. Add the all-purpose flour, vanilla, and lemon zest. Mix on low speed just to combine, then set aside.

FOR THE CRUST AND FILLING

Preheat the oven to 375°F.

Bake the crust until it is lightly golden and the bottom is set, 10 minutes. This will prevent the bottom from getting soggy.

Fill the pie crust with the room-temperature frangipane and spread it in an even layer.

Combine the sliced stone fruit with the sugar in a large bowl, and leave to marinate for 5–10 minutes. Press the fruit into the frangipane, but make sure to leave some fruit poking through.

Place the tart on a rimmed baking sheet to catch any spillage and bake until the frangipane has risen and almost engulfed the fruit, about 40 minutes. The top of the frangipane should be slightly golden.

Allow to cool completely then brush with melted butter, dust with crushed pistachios and icing sugar, and serve with some crème fraîche on the side (if using).

Note

The frangipane can be made ahead and refrigerated in an airtight container up to 1 day in advance, but bring it to room temperature before using.

SEB SAYS

If the crust browns too quickly, don't panic! Just lower the oven temperature to 350°F and cover the edges of the crust loosely with aluminum foil.

3

**PULLING
OUT ALL
THE STOPS**

As the summer winds down and the evenings turn brisk, we realize that we only have a limited number of opportunities left to entertain outdoors with the backdrop of fall colors, so we like to take full advantage. We've already hosted so many spring- and summer-inspired meals together and now we get to enjoy one last outdoor meal before packing away the outdoor furniture and moving inside for winter entertaining by the fire.

And celebrating all that is fall with a harvest linner is the perfect way to welcome the change of season. If you opt for delicate, seasonal courses along with a few body-warming cocktails, a fall harvest meal is the ideal transition meal for this time of year as you embrace the arrival of the cooler days and settle into meals with heartier menus.

Unlike many of our dinner parties, a fall harvest–inspired meal can be enjoyed any time of day, but since there are only so many weekend nights, and to avoid having to pick a date several weeks in advance, we suggest hosting this meal as a late lunch/early dinner.

We start our linner around 2:00 pm and aim to have everyone seated at the table to enjoy their meals roughly one hour later. This timing is great for a Sunday afternoon, so your guests can linger until the early evening hours but get home early enough to get a good night's sleep for the week ahead.

FALL HARVEST LINNER

SETTING

If you live in the city like we do, it can be challenging to create the ideal ambience for a fall harvest setting, although it's not impossible. While the party in this chapter took place at our friends Tim and Laurie's farm, you can easily take inspiration from this picturesque environment and incorporate many of the same elements into a city setting.

For this meal, our goal is to set a casual yet proper table, while being as sustainable as possible. For example, instead of buying out-of-season flowers, we like to use fresh garden florals that need to be cut back shortly for the winter anyway. We take greenery, berry branches, and the last few blossoms of hydrangeas and combine them to match the look of our table.

When it comes to setting the table, we use tableware in an antique blue-and-white pattern for a slightly more elegant feel. Using a more traditional pattern works especially well when you incorporate rustic elements, like the rattan chargers and natural grayed wood table, since it balances out the overall look. We also love the matching vases in blue and white, along with a few basic white cubes, scattered along the center of the table, to hold our cut garden florals.

One challenge you might encounter while entertaining outdoors in the fall is managing the early sunset, which creates the need for lighting as early as 5:00 pm in some places. Instead of using lots of small candles to light up your table, try experimenting with string lights. For this DIY trick, all you'll need to do is find three or four clear, empty alcohol bottles and thread one or two thin strands of battery operated string lights down through the neck of the bottles right to the base. These battery operated string lights will have a small switch on them, which you can leave hanging out of the bottle top or tape down to the outside of the bottle for a cleaner look like we did. Whether you have the luxury of hosting your fall harvest dinner at a farm or you're hosting in your backyard in the city, this two-minute trick can give your table a glow as you move into the early evening.

SHEILA SAYS

If you have the luxury of your own garden, use vegetables from your final harvest in these recipes! Fresh veggies from your garden make a fantastic take-home gift for your guests too.

Since the central idea of this meal is to celebrate having one more chance to entertain outdoors, the first few canapés are meant to be enjoyed while standing and mingling. For this reason, they are prepared in bite-sized portions.

The first canapé is a Beet + Feta Stack. For this dish, make sure to use small beets to keep it bite-sized. The second canapé we are serving is Chili Maple Nuts. This recipe is one of the easiest to make since the entire dish can be prepared in a single skillet. If you want to save yourself some time, you can make this dish up to 1 week ahead of your party. If they're stored in an airtight container, the nuts should actually last for up to 2 weeks. We like to serve them in one large bowl with a serving spoon and stack a number of smaller individual bowls for guests to fill themselves. This avoids anyone reaching into the nuts with their fingers.

Once the canapés are done, it's time for the seated portion of your meal. Playing on the fall inspiration, Carrot + Apple Soup with Sautéed Mushrooms is the perfect way to start. Unlike more traditional fall soups, this one is extremely light and won't fill your guests up.

Next, it's time for some greens. Instead of serving a traditional salad, we offer a composed fall salad: Fig, Gorgonzola + Walnut Salad with Honey Balsamic Vinaigrette. The key to this dish is presentation. Try spreading out the crostini and radicchio leaves to create the base, then add the other lettuces and ingredients, topping it all off with a spoonful of dressing.

The main course is Cornish Hen, served with Roasted Root Vegetables and Sweet Potato Mash. At this point in the meal, your guests might not have much room for dessert, so we recommend serving a small on-theme course like Poached Oranges with Honey or a small slice of Chocolate Fondant Cake. Both of these dishes take a bit of time to prepare, so bear that in mind when you're doing your prep.

WHAT'S ON THE MENU

WHAT'S ON THE BAR

For our fall harvest linner we offer a few cocktails for our guests to enjoy while they nibble on canapés. They can also bring them to the table for the seated portion of the meal.

Our first cocktail, Fall Sangria, is a batched one. It is easily prepared in advance and incorporates fall fruits like apples and pears. To add some additional fall flavor to this recipe, we use full sticks of cinnamon. We recommend you try it with and without the cinnamon to see which version you like best.

As you'll know by now, batched cocktails are a go-to item for us because they mean we don't have to mix up individual cocktails all night, but if you're up for it, we have two other recommended cocktails that are perfectly suited to a fall harvest linner.

The Cider Sidecar features apple cider, cognac, and Cointreau, once again playing off some fall fruit flavors. Mixed in the traditional method of a martini, the theatrics of shaking one of these drinks up will always bring a smile to your guests' faces.

Lastly, one of our personal favorite cocktails: Sage-Fig Rum Punch. Not only does this cocktail look beautiful, but its fresh yet herbal taste acts as the perfect complement to both the spiced nuts and the courses served throughout the meal.

FALL HARVEST LINNER

COCKTAILS

FALL SANGRIA (P240)

CIDER SIDECAR (P240)

SAGE-FIG RUM PUNCH (P241)

CANAPÉS

BEET + FETA STACKS (P243)

CHILI MAPLE NUTS (P243)

FIRST COURSE

CARROT + APPLE SOUP WITH SAUTÉED MUSHROOMS (P245)

SECOND COURSE

FIG, GORGONZOLA + WALNUT SALAD WITH HONEY BALSAMIC VINAIGRETTE (P246)

MAIN COURSE

CORNISH HEN (P249)

SWEET POTATO MASH (P250)

ROASTED ROOT VEGETABLES (P251)

DESSERT

SYRUP-POACHED ORANGES (P252)

CHOCOLATE FONDANT CAKE (P252)

PARTY COUNTDOWN:

FALL HARVEST LINNER

3 THREE DAYS BEFORE

- ○ Send a reminder email or text to your guests with details about the event.

- ○ Check the weather forecast! Fall weather can be unpredictable and you want to be sure your linner won't get rained out. Remind your guests they'll be dining outside so they dress appropriately.

- ○ Prepare the chili maple nuts and store them in an airtight container.

- ○ Make your grocery and alcohol list. This menu has three delicious cocktails but each one needs a variety of ingredients you will want to shop for in advance.

- ○ Check you have enough plates and glasses for your guests.

2 TWO DAYS BEFORE

- ○ Grocery shop and stock up at the liquor store.

- ○ Prepare the soup. Refrigerate in an airtight container.

- ○ Prep the beets and feta. Refrigerate the feta mixture in an airtight container. Roast the beets and refrigerate them whole in an airtight container. All that's left on the day of is to slice the beets and stack!

- ○ Buy the vegetables for the DIY baskets.

TIME-SAVING TIPS

If you can't find mini shopping baskets for the DIY place setting, use small paper lunch bags or burlap sacks. Also, just resting a mini pumpkin on each place setting would suffice if you don't have fresh vegetables available.

Include durable vegetables like squash and carrots in your DIY basket. They will last longer in your fridge, which means you can prep them several days in advance.

We've provided two dishes that complement each other superbly for the dessert, but feel free to pick only one to simplify the preparation. We promise your guests won't know!

1 THE DAY BEFORE

○ Prep all the vegetables that will be served alongside the Cornish hen. Since this is a linner, you'll have fewer hours to prep on the day of the event.

○ Prepare the poached oranges and refrigerate in an airtight container.

○ Have a few shawls or light blankets rolled up and at the ready in case the temperature drops.

0 THE DAY OF

○ Set the table.

○ Assemble the DIY baskets.

○ Assemble the beet and feta stacks.

○ Plate the salad and have the dressing set aside in a bottle, ready to be shaken and drizzled over each salad.

○ Make the sweet potato mash (you can prepare it in the morning and reheat it in the afternoon) and roast the Cornish hens and the vegetables.

○ Bake the chocolate fondant cake right before it is served or, if you anticipate being in a time-crunch, you can make the cake earlier in the day or even the night before and store it, covered on a cake stand, at room temperature.

FALL SANGRIA

COCKTAILS

FALL SANGRIA

yield: makes 6–8 cocktails · prep time: 20 minutes

Ingredients

1 (750 ml) bottle sweet white wine, chilled

1 cup apple cider

1 apple (honeycrisp, Granny Smith, and ambrosia all work well), sliced in ¼-inch-thick rounds

1 bosc pear, sliced into ¼-inch-thick wedges

¼ cup pomegranate seeds

1 (750 ml) bottle sparkling wine or prosecco, chilled

2 rosemary sprigs or 3 cinnamon sticks, for garnish

Method

Place the wine and cider in a large pitcher. Add the sliced apples, sliced pears, and pomegranate seeds. Top with the sparkling wine, and stir gently to mix. Garnish with the rosemary or cinnamon (but not both).

CIDER SIDECAR

yield: makes 1 cocktail · prep time: 5 minutes

Ingredients

¼ cup apple cider

2 oz cognac

1 oz Cointreau

2 Tbsp lemon juice

1 strip lemon zest, for garnish

1 brandied cherry, for garnish

Method

Place the cider, cognac, Cointreau, and lemon juice in a cocktail shaker filled with ice. Shake vigorously. Strain into a martini glass and garnish with the lemon zest and cherry.

SAGE-FIG RUM PUNCH

yield: makes 1 cocktail · prep time: 5 minutes

Ingredients

2 oz white rum
1 oz Grand Marnier
2 Tbsp sage-infused simple syrup (see note)
½ lemon, juice of
Club soda
½ fig, for garnish

Method

Place the rum, Grand Marnier, simple syrup, and lemon juice in a stemmed rocks glass filled with ice, then stir gently to combine.

Top with club soda and garnish with the fig.

NOTE

To make sage-infused simple syrup, follow the method on page 112 for the thyme-infused simple syrup, but replace the thyme with 4 sprigs of fresh sage.

BEET + FETA
STACKS

CHILI MAPLE
NUTS

BEET + FETA STACKS

yield: serves 6–8 · prep time: 30 minutes · cook time: 45 minutes

Ingredients

4 medium beets, washed
1 cup crumbled feta cheese
¼ cup brick-style cream cheese
Black pepper
Honey, olive oil, and grated lemon zest, for garnish, optional

Method

Place the beets in a pot and cover with cold water by 2 inches. Bring to a boil over high heat, reduce the heat, and simmer, uncovered, until the beets are fork-tender, about 45 minutes. Drain and let cool completely.

In a large mixing bowl, mix together the feta cheese, cream cheese, and pepper to taste with a spoon or handheld mixer.

Slice the beets into rounds about ¼-inch thick, or use a 1-inch cookie cutter to make perfect circles. You should wind up with about 60 rounds.

Using your hands, roll ½ tsp of the feta mixture into a ball and place it on a beet round. Place another beet round on top and gently press together. Place another feta ball on top, followed by another beet round, and gently press together. Secure the layers with a short skewer or toothpick. Repeat until all the beet rounds have been used.

Garnish with a drizzle of honey and olive oil and a sprinkling of lemon zest (if using). Serve immediately or refrigerate for up to 2 hours.

CHILI MAPLE NUTS

yield: makes 3 cups · prep time: 5 minutes · cook time: 10 minutes

Ingredients

1 tsp olive oil
2 garlic cloves, minced
½ tsp chili flakes
½ tsp smoked paprika
½ tsp black pepper
½ cup walnut halves
½ cup pecan halves
½ cup cashews
½ cup hazelnuts
½ cup whole almonds
½ cup dried cherries
½ cup maple syrup
2 tsp sea salt

Method

Heat a large skillet over medium-high heat, then add the oil, garlic, and chili flakes. Cook, stirring constantly, until the garlic is golden and fragrant, about 30 seconds.

Stir in the paprika and pepper. Add the walnuts, pecans, cashews, hazelnuts, almonds, and cherries, and stir continuously for about 3 minutes so that all the nuts are coated in the oil.

Pour the maple syrup over the nuts, turn off the heat, and continue to stir until the nuts are evenly coated in the syrup, about 5 minutes.

Add the salt, stir to combine, and transfer the nut mixture to a baking sheet lined with parchment paper to cool.

Note

These nuts can be made ahead and stored in an airtight container for up to 2 weeks.

CARROT + APPLE SOUP WITH SAUTÉED MUSHROOMS

yield: serves 6–8 · prep time: 15 minutes · cook time: 35 minutes

Ingredients

SOUP
1½ lb heirloom carrots
3 large green apples
1 small yellow onion
2 garlic cloves
¼ cup olive oil
½ tsp ground ginger
6 cups vegetable stock
2 thyme sprigs
Sea salt and black pepper

MUSHROOMS
2 Tbsp olive oil + more for drizzling
2 (each 12 oz) packages sliced
    mixed mushrooms (cremini,
    oyster, etc.)
Sea salt

Method

FOR THE SOUP
Preheat the oven to 375°F. Line a baking sheet with parchment paper.

Peel and cut the carrots, apples, and onion into approximately 2-inch pieces. Coarsely chop the garlic.

Place the carrots, apple, onion, and garlic on the prepared baking sheet. Add the oil and ginger and toss to coat. Bake until the carrots and onions soften and begin to caramelize, about 20 minutes.

Bring the stock and thyme to a boil in a large stockpot over medium-high heat. Once the stock is boiling, remove the thyme and add the roasted vegetables. Reduce the heat to medium-low and simmer, uncovered, until the carrots are soft, about 10 minutes.

FOR THE MUSHROOMS
Heat the oil in a medium skillet set over medium-high heat. Add the mushrooms and stir to coat in the oil. Cook until the mushrooms are dark and crispy, about 5 minutes, then season to taste with salt.

TO FINISH
Remove the soup from the heat, let cool slightly, then transfer to a blender and purée until smooth. Season to taste with salt and pepper.

Serve with the sautéed mushrooms overtop along with a drizzle of oil.

FIG, GORGONZOLA + WALNUT SALAD WITH HONEY BALSAMIC VINAIGRETTE

yield: serves 6–8 · prep time: 30 minutes

Ingredients

DRESSING

½ cup olive oil

2 Tbsp honey

2 Tbsp balsamic vinegar

1 shallot, finely chopped

1 garlic clove, minced

1 Tbsp cold water

Sea salt and black pepper

SALAD

2 heads radicchio

12 crostini

2 heads Boston lettuce

8 fresh figs

12 oz gorgonzola, broken into large pieces

1 cup walnut halves, toasted, optional

Sea salt and black pepper

Method

FOR THE DRESSING

In a small bowl, whisk all the dressing ingredients until emulsified. Refrigerate in an airtight container for up to 2 days.

FOR THE SALAD

Prepare the radicchio and Boston lettuce by cutting the bottom stems off and removing the wilted, torn, or bruised outside leaves. Peel away the whole leaves, leaving them intact, trimming the bottom as needed, and set aside.

Cut large figs into 6 wedges and smaller figs into 4.

Divide the whole radicchio leaves and crostini equally among the plates and place the Boston lettuce on top. Divide the gorgonzola, figs, and walnuts (if using) equally among the plates as well.

Season lightly with salt and pepper, drizzle dressing overtop, and serve immediately.

CORNISH HEN

yield: serves 6–8 · prep time: 15 minutes · cook time: 30–45 minutes

Ingredients

5 garlic cloves, minced

2½ tsp sweet paprika

5 tsp herbes de Provence

½ tsp sea salt

2½ tsp black pepper

2½ Tbsp olive oil

4 Cornish hens

1 Tbsp grated lemon zest

1 Tbsp flat-leaf parsley,
    finely chopped

Method

Preheat the oven to 350°F.

In a small bowl, combine the garlic, paprika, herbes de Provence, salt, pepper, and oil to form a paste. Set aside.

Pat dry the Cornish hens with paper towels. Cut them along the breast and backbone to halve them—keep in mind, this is different than spatchcocking. There are some excellent videos on YouTube on how to do this.

Rub the hens with the seasoning paste.

Heat a large cast iron pan on the stove over high heat. Sear the Cornish hens, skin side down, until the skin is crisp and releases easily from the pan, 3–4 minutes.

Transfer the hens to a large baking sheet or dish and let cool enough to handle. Push the drumstick meat down the bone by about 1 inch. (When you're serving these with the sweet potato mash, this will give the fancy effect of showing the bone sticking straight up on the plate.)

Cook the Cornish hens until their internal temperature is at least 160°F, but not more than 180°F. The timing can range from 25 to 40 minutes, depending on the size of the hens, so use a meat thermometer to be sure.

Remove the hens from the oven and sprinkle with the lemon zest and chopped parsley. Reserve the cooking juices. See the serving instructions on page 251.

SWEET POTATO MASH

yield: serves 6–8 · prep time: 20 minutes + 20 minutes to cool · cook time: 1 hour 5 minutes

Ingredients

4 large sweet potatoes

4 large Yukon gold potatoes, peeled and cut into 2-inch pieces

½ cup butter

1 cup whipping (36%) cream

2 tsp white pepper

Ground nutmeg

½ cup sour cream

2 Tbsp maple syrup

Sea salt

Method

Preheat the oven to 350°F. Line a baking sheet with parchment paper.

Place the sweet potatoes on the baking sheet and roast until they can be easily pierced with a small knife, about 45 minutes. Let cool enough to handle, about 20 minutes, then slice each one lengthwise, scoop the flesh into a medium bowl, and set aside. Discard the skins.

Meanwhile, in a medium pot, cover the Yukon gold potatoes with cold water by about 2 inches and bring to a boil over high heat. Reduce the heat to medium and simmer, uncovered, until the potatoes are soft but retain their shape, about 20 minutes. Drain into a colander and add to the bowl with the sweet potatoes.

Place both potatoes, butter, cream, pepper, and a pinch of nutmeg in a stand mixer fitted with the paddle attachment and mix on medium speed until evenly blended. Add the sour cream and maple syrup, and beat on high speed until smooth. Season to taste with salt and transfer to an oven-safe dish large enough to hold everything snugly but without crowding. (If you want to make this mash a few hours ahead, you can cover it with foil and reheat in a 350°F oven until hot, about 20 minutes.) See the serving instructions on page 251.

ROASTED ROOT VEGETABLES

yield: serves 6–8 · prep time: 20 minutes · cook time: 45 minutes

Ingredients

1 lb Brussels sprouts

1 lb heirloom carrots

2 cups red or white pearl onions

2 Tbsp thyme leaves

2 Tbsp rosemary leaves

1 tsp ground fennel seeds

½ cup olive oil

1 cup fresh or frozen and thawed cranberries

Sea salt and black pepper

Method

Preheat the oven to 350°F. Line a baking sheet with parchment paper.

Stem and halve the Brussels sprouts, peel and cut the carrots into 2-inch pieces, peel the onions, and coarsely chop the thyme and rosemary. Transfer the vegetables and herbs to a medium bowl and add the fennel seeds and oil, mixing well to coat evenly.

Transfer the vegetables to the prepared baking sheet and roast until the vegetables are caramelized and can be easily pierced with a knife, about 35 minutes.

Increase the oven temperature to 375°F and sprinkle the cranberries over the vegetables. Roast for 10 more minutes.

Remove from the oven, season to taste with salt and pepper, and mix well to ensure the seasoning is distributed throughout.

ASSEMBLY FOR CORNISH HEN, SWEET POTATO MASH + ROASTED FALL VEGETABLES

Place a large spoonful of the sweet potato mash on a large dinner plate. Place a Cornish hen half directly in the center of the plate, straddling the mash. Arrange the vegetables around the Cornish hen and pour the reserved cooking juices from the Cornish hen all around.

SYRUP-POACHED ORANGES

yield: serves 6 · prep time: 20 minutes · cook time: 40 minutes

Ingredients

6 Valencia oranges (or other
   thin-skinned orange, not navel)
5 cups granulated sugar
4 cinnamon sticks
8 green cardamom pods
½ tsp whole cloves
2 Tbsp cognac, optional

Method

Completely peel the oranges, removing as much of the stringy pith as possible.

Place the oranges in a large stockpot, then add cold water to cover them by 1 inch. Add the sugar, cinnamon, cardamom pods, and cloves. Stir once, then bring to a boil, uncovered and without stirring, over high heat.

Once boiling, reduce the heat to a simmer, add the cognac (if using), and cook until the oranges are soft and feel heavy when lifted with a spoon (this means they have absorbed the syrup), 30–40 minutes.

Serve the oranges warm, or refrigerate them in the syrup in an airtight container for up to 3 days and serve cool.

CHOCOLATE FONDANT CAKE

yield: serves 6–8 · prep time: 20 minutes · cook time: 20 minutes

Ingredients

1 cup butter
7 oz dark chocolate (at least
   70% cocoa)
5 large eggs, room temperature
1⅔ cups icing sugar
1 Tbsp all-purpose flour

Method

Preheat the oven to 375°F. Line the bottom of a 9-inch springform pan with silicone or parchment paper. Coat the sides of the pan and the parchment paper with cooking spray.

Fill a medium saucepan with water and bring to a simmer over medium-high heat. Set a mixing bowl on top to create a double boiler. Ensure that the bottom of the bowl doesn't touch the water.

Place the butter and chocolate in the mixing bowl and stir gently and consistently until melted and combined.

Remove the bowl from the heat and allow to cool for about 5 minutes, stirring occasionally.

Once cooled, add the eggs, one at a time, whisking quickly and vigorously until they are fully combined— this will help prevent them from cooking in the warm chocolate.

Stir in the icing sugar and flour until just combined. Pour the batter into the prepared pan.

Bake until the top of the cake is set but the center is still soft and wobbly, about 15 minutes. Allow the cake to cool slightly before removing from the pan and serving. This can be served warm or made earlier in the day and stored at room temperature. If you make this more than a few hours ahead, keep the cake refrigerated and remove from the fridge 15 minutes before serving to allow it to come to room temperature.

3

**PULLING
OUT ALL
THE STOPS**

TIP *When you're placing
items like bacon, sausage,
and French toast in the oven
to keep them warm, cover
them tightly with aluminum
foil to keep them from drying
out. If you decide to serve
classic scrambled or fried
eggs, keep these to be prepared à la minute.*

While it is our tradition to host a big brunch on Christmas morning for our family, we believe brunch shouldn't be just an annual event. We love to host weekend brunches because they are a more relaxed method of entertaining and make an ordinary Saturday or Sunday feel special.

Weather permitting, we recommend hosting brunch outdoors whenever possible. There's something refreshing about eating in the garden surrounded by fresh air and gorgeous greenery. But if you're hosting in the winter or the weather isn't cooperating with your plans, there's nothing wrong with setting up your brunch indoors.

When we're planning a brunch, we live by the saying "the more the merrier." Whether it's neighbors who hosted you a while back, or friends you haven't seen in a long time, brunch is the perfect opportunity to host people of all different ages and interests. The other nice thing about brunch is that it's simple to prepare. That doesn't mean it isn't a fair amount of work, though, which is why we've included it in this section.

However, don't let us stress you out. Most of the items can be prepared ahead of time, and by serving brunch buffet-style, you alleviate the pressure that comes with constantly serving and clearing plates. Mixtures and batters can be made the night before and anything hot can be prepared before your guests arrive and left in the oven to keep warm until you're ready to serve. By the time your guests arrive, all that will be left to do is set up the buffet!

SUNDAY BRUNCHIN'

SHEILA SAYS *Have an extra set of plates and cutlery ready in case your guests want to switch to a clean plate after having French toast or pancakes with syrup. It will encourage them to keep going back for more without bothering you or the rest of the table.*

SETTING

Even though brunch is supposed to be a casual meal, the table can still be set with a white linen tablecloth to add a touch of formality. Even though the meal is not fancy, we invite our guests to dress up a little, and we add some elegant touches to make the event feel special.

Since brunch can be a meal for guests of all ages, we like to use a roll of chalkboard paper as our table runner and provide each guest with a piece of chalk or even a small cup of colored chalks. The runner makes a great canvas for fun and games for our guests and can also be used as a replacement for traditional place cards. Simply write the name of each guest in front of each place setting and let your guests know to hunt for their name before taking a seat at the table.

To match the tablecloth, use everyday white plateware and basic silverware. To give our table that extra little pop and bit of elegance, we like to bring out our beautiful crystal glassware. While we aren't afraid to risk our nice glassware around a crowd of all ages, you might prefer to give younger guests glasses that are more easily replaced. Finally, to help tie the whole table setting together and add a touch of whimsical fun, place tiny pink florals and cupcakes at each place setting. All the food will be served buffet-style on the counter, so don't worry about leaving space on your table for large platters. When you start your setup, use sticky notes to keep track of what you will be serving on each platter. This is especially helpful for this meal since there are so many components. It also makes it easier for your kitchen helpers to know what will be served where.

Even though all the food for this meal will be set up buffet-style, each dish should still be strategically placed so your guests don't miss anything while they're working their way down the counter. We recommend grouping each dish by type: first the hot food, then seafood, cheeses, breads, salads, fruits, and sweets. You can also scatter a few vases throughout the buffet and by your prosecco bar to tie the décor together.

Keep garnishes near the items they are meant for: butter and syrup near the French toast, etc.

Use serving platters and stands that will give your buffet spread different levels. Place platters on top of small boxes or short glasses to act as risers and give the presentation some height.

SEB SAYS *The first thing I like to do when we decide to host a brunch is count how many small and large plates we have, since we find that people go through more plates at a buffet than at a sit-down meal. You don't want to run short and have to break out disposable plates. Doing this well in advance allows you time to shop for a few extra things if necessary.*

WHAT'S ON THE MENU

Instead of coursing out the dishes like we have for almost every other meal in this book, all the dishes for this meal should be served at the same time on the buffet bar. Here's how we set it up: First, we start with the hot foods. They're the main attraction of any brunch, so we like to create excitement by starting off the buffet with the foods that our guests will want to eat first. Instead of serving scrambled or fried eggs, we like to add some versatility to our buffet by serving a frittata, which could also be presented as a quiche if you pour the egg mixture directly into a thawed frozen pie crust and bake according to the package instructions. We also serve deviled eggs since they make a nice room-temperature addition to the buffet that can be enjoyed on their own or added to one of the salads.

Some other items that should be included in the hot foods section are the French Toast and the meats. Maple syrup is an obvious must-serve alongside French toast, but many hosts forget to offer thinly sliced pats of butter and some berries on the side as well.

The next section we like to plate is our seafood. Thinly sliced smoked salmon and shrimp cocktail are always a big hit at our weekend brunches, so make sure you have more than enough seafood to feed all your guests with some left over.

Next, it's time for our cheeses. While the variety of cheeses you should offer depends largely on the number of guests you're hosting, we recommend putting together a cheese board with at least three or four different cheeses. Make sure to include some more traditional cheeses, like cream cheese and feta.

When it comes to breads, you should have some pre-toasted basic breads and bagels ready to serve, but we also like to include a small platter of the still trendy and always popular avocado toast. You don't need to prepare enough for every guest to have a full serving but it will help add a bit of color to your bread section.

Next come the salads. We like to offer a Caesar Salad and Simple Green Salad for brunch. Both are easy to make and pair well with the other options. Consider keeping the dressings in small pitchers or bowls with spoons so guests can dress their own salads to their liking.

In our fruits and veggies section we include two well-constructed plates with substantial variety. While you may have to do some additional shopping for your veggie plate, most of the fruits you'll be including on your fruit platter can also be used as the fruit garnish for the prosecco/juice bar!

Finally, the last section of our brunch buffet is always our sweets section. The assortment needed at this station is also dictated by the number of guests you'll be entertaining. Some combination of chocolate, cookies, candy, and cake is sure to satisfy your guests' collective sweet tooth as they finish their plates and get ready to enjoy the rest of their Sunday.

WHAT'S ON THE BAR

In the spirit of the buffet, we offer a few beverage stations for easy self-service.

Since you'll probably be hosting brunch in the late morning, many of your guests will still want coffee. A coffee and tea station is going to see a lot of action! We like to get creative with our coffee and tea accompaniments. Rather than leaving the milk and cream in cartons beside the coffee pot and tea kettle, we pour them into clear mini pitchers that we keep on ice at the end of the buffet. Label the pitchers so your guests don't mix up the different types of milk or cream.

In addition to the coffee and tea station, we always include a prosecco and juice bar. Place two or three bottles of prosecco in a large champagne bucket on ice and serve a few different juices in pitchers for easy pouring. If you're looking to add a touch of formality or some extra flavor, add small bowls of berries that your guests can use as garnishes. Before choosing your juices and berries, consider whether they pair well with prosecco for anyone who might be interested in making a mimosa.

Classic juices that pair well with prosecco include orange, pink grapefruit, and peach but also try some variations like lychee or pear.

SUNDAY BRUNCHIN'

BRUNCH BUFFET (P267)

ALMOND MILK RICE PUDDING (P270)

DEVILED EGGS (P270)

FRENCH TOAST (P271)

AVOCADO TOAST (P271)

SIMPLE GREEN SALAD (P273)

CAESAR SALAD (P273)

LEEK + MUSHROOM FRITTATA
(WITH QUICHE VARIATION) (P274)

PARTY COUNTDOWN:

SUNDAY BRUNCHIN'

3 THREE DAYS BEFORE

○ Send a reminder email or text to your guests with details about the brunch.

○ Do an inventory of your plates and platters, and use sticky notes to remind you what dish goes where.

○ Decide where you'll set up the buffet. You want guests to be able to move along in one direction.

○ Make your grocery and alcohol lists.

2 TWO DAYS BEFORE

○ Grocery shop and stock up at the liquor store.

○ Take out all your serving platters and dishes, then use sticky notes to keep track of which course is being served in which dish.

○ Fill jars with candies and sweets. They can sit on the counter as long as the jars are sealed.

*Use store-bought cocktail sauce and
frozen, pre-cooked shrimp.*

1 THE DAY BEFORE

○ Set the table.

○ Prepare the batter for the French toast.

○ Make the almond milk rice pudding.

○ Prepare the deviled eggs (keep the yolk
mixture separate from the whites and just
pipe them in the morning).

○ Prepare the fruits and veggies. Refrigerate
in airtight containers.

○ Prep all the cheeses (cream cheese, feta,
and cheese board) the night before, place
them on their serving platter, cover tightly,
and refrigerate.

0 THE DAY OF

○ Cook the bacon and sausage.

○ Cook the frittata (if you're sticking with
scrambled or fried eggs, cook them right
before serving).

○ Cook the French toast.

DEVILED EGGS

BRUNCH BUFFET

BRUNCH BUFFET

yield: serves 6–8 · prep time: 60–90 minutes (depending on how many options you serve)

MEAT + SEAFOOD

Ingredients
1 lb bacon
1 lb sausages (pork or turkey)
1 lb cold-smoked salmon (lox)
1 lb poached shrimp (1 16/20 count)
6 oz cocktail sauce

Method
Fry bacon on the barbecue for 3 minutes per side.

Fry sausages on the barbecue for 2–4 minutes per side, depending on size.

Form salmon into rosettes and place on a platter.

Buy pre-cooked or poach the shrimp (see method on page 293). Serve with the cocktail sauce.

BREADS

Ingredients
3 pita breads
Rye toast
6 bagels

Method
Cut pita into triangles and place on a platter.

Toast a few slices of the rye bread used for the Avocado Toast (page 271) and serve plain.

Halve and arrange bagels on a platter.

CRUDITÉS

Ingredients
1 red onion, thinly sliced
1 English cucumber, thinly sliced
3 field tomatoes, thinly sliced
3 avocados

Method
Slice and arrange on a platter just before serving.
Squeeze lemon juice on the avocado to prevent browning.

FRUIT

Ingredients
1 pint strawberries
1 pint raspberries
1 pint blueberries

Method
Remove the strawberry hulls and arrange in a bowl or on a platter with the raspberries and blueberries.

DAIRY

Ingredients
9 oz cream cheese
14 oz feta cheese
1 lb various cheeses
1 stick butter

Method
Arrange cream cheese in a small bowl.

Place feta on a platter.

Use whatever you like to assemble a cheese board—brie, havarti, and cheddar all work well at brunch.

Leave butter out overnight to soften for easier spreading.

SWEETS

Ingredients
1 cup chocolates (Turtles, OMG Clusters, or another variety)
1 cup candy (jelly beans, gummy bears, sour cherries, yogurt-covered raisins)
6–8 cookies (chocolate chip, plus another variety)

Method
Place the chocolates, candy, and cookies on a large platter. You could put smaller candies, such as gummy bears, in small bowls.

LEFT

BERRIES,
COOKIES,
ALMOND MILK
RICE PUDDING

TOP

BACON, SAUSAGE,
FRENCH TOAST

BOTTOM

AVOCADO TOAST

ALMOND MILK RICE PUDDING

yield: serves 6–8 · prep time: 10 minutes · cook time: 25 minutes

Ingredients

½ cup Arborio rice
2⅓ cups almond milk
½ tsp almond extract
½ tsp vanilla extract
Sea salt
1 cup each dried coconut, pistachios, raisins, dried currants, for topping

Method

Rinse the rice under cold running water until the water runs clear.

Bring the almond milk to a boil in a medium saucepan over medium-high heat. Add the rice, reduce the heat to low, cover, and simmer, stirring occasionally to make sure the rice doesn't stick to the bottom of the pot, until thick and creamy, about 15 minutes. Stir in the almond and vanilla extracts and a pinch of salt. Cover and let rest off the heat for about 5 minutes. Spoon into small 4–6 oz mason jars and let your guests add their preferred toppings.

DEVILED EGGS

yield: serves 6–8 · prep time: 40 minutes

Ingredients

⅓ cup nonfat plain Greek yogurt
2 tsp smooth Dijon mustard
1 tsp white vinegar
1 Tbsp kosher salt
¾ tsp curry powder
¼ tsp dry mustard powder
⅛ tsp cayenne pepper
6 eggs, hard-boiled and peeled
2 tsp sweet or smoked paprika
Chopped chives, for garnish

Method

In a medium glass bowl, stir together the yogurt, Dijon, vinegar, salt, curry powder, dry mustard, and cayenne pepper.

Cut the eggs in half lengthwise. With a small spoon, gently scoop out the yolks and add them to the bowl with the yogurt mixture. Mash the yolks into the filling with the back of a fork until smooth. For a very smooth filling, press the egg yolks through a sieve and into the bowl.

Scoop or pipe the egg yolk mixture into the egg whites. Refrigerate until ready to serve.

Just before serving, sprinkle with paprika and chives. Leftover deviled eggs will keep in an airtight container in the fridge for up to 2 days.

FRENCH TOAST

yield: serves 6–8 · prep time: 15 minutes ·
cook time: 10 minutes per batch

Ingredients

6 eggs
¾ cup milk
2 tsp vanilla extract
¾ tsp cinnamon
Ground nutmeg
1 loaf white or whole wheat
    sliced sandwich bread
Orange slices, for garnish
Raspberries, for garnish
Icing sugar, for garnish
Maple syrup, for serving

Method

In a large, wide bowl, beat the eggs with the milk,
vanilla, cinnamon, and a pinch of nutmeg. Dip each
slice of bread into the egg mixture, turning to coat
both sides evenly.

Heat a large, lightly greased, nonstick skillet over
medium heat, and cook the bread until browned on
both sides, about 5 minutes per side. (You'll
likely have to cook it in batches to avoid overcrowding your pan.) If you're not serving it immediately,
transfer to a baking dish and wrap with aluminum
foil. Place it in the oven on the "Keep Warm" setting
(usually 150°F) for up to 2 hours.

When you're ready to serve, place the warmed dish
on a trivet right on the buffet, or transfer the French
toast to a platter. Place the orange slices, raspberries, icing sugar, and maple syrup alongside for
guests to help themselves.

AVOCADO TOAST

yield: serves 6–8 · prep time: 15 minutes

Ingredients

5 ripe avocados
½ tsp sea salt
Garlic powder
2 Tbsp olive oil
2 Tbsp cream cheese,
    room temperature
2 tsp lemon juice
8 slices rye bread, toasted

Method

Place the avocados, salt, a pinch of garlic powder,
the oil, cream cheese, and lemon juice in a food processor fitted with the steel blade and blend until
light and fluffy. Refrigerate in an airtight container
for no more than 2 hours—it spoils fairly quickly, so
don't make it too far ahead of serving.

When you're ready to serve, spread the avocado
mixture on the toast. Serve on your buffet table near
the fresh veggies and cheeses for guests to garnish
according to taste.

SIMPLE GREEN SALAD

yield: serves 6–8 · prep time: 10 minutes

Ingredients
6 cups mixed greens
1 lemon, juice of
3 Tbsp olive oil
Sea salt

Method
Place all the ingredients in a bowl and toss just before serving.

Note
You can serve the lemon juice and oil mixed together in a small jar beside the bowl of greens so that guests can dress their own salad to their liking and the salad doesn't get soggy.

CAESAR SALAD

yield: serves 6–8 · prep time: 15 minutes

Ingredients
DRESSING
2 small garlic cloves, minced
½ cup grated parmigiano-reggiano cheese
1 cup mayonnaise
2 Tbsp lemon juice
1 tsp anchovy paste or 1 minced anchovy
1 tsp Dijon mustard
1 tsp Worcestershire sauce
¼ tsp kosher salt
¼ tsp black pepper

SALAD
1 head romaine lettuce
1 cup croutons
½ cup grated parmigiano-reggiano cheese

Method
FOR THE DRESSING
Combine all the dressing ingredients in a mason jar and shake until emulsified. Refrigerate for up to 1 week.

FOR THE SALAD
Place the lettuce, croutons, and parmigiano-reggiano in a large bowl. You can use ¼ cup of dressing if you'd like to dress the whole salad, or you can leave the dressing in a small jar on the side so that guests can dress their own.

LEEK + MUSHROOM FRITTATA
(WITH QUICHE VARIATION)

yield: serves 6–8 · prep time: 20 minutes · cook time: 20 minutes (45 minutes for quiche)

Ingredients

2 Tbsp butter

1 leek, white and light green parts only, chopped

12 oz sliced cremini and/or oyster mushrooms

Sea salt and black pepper

10 eggs

2 cups shredded gruyère cheese + extra for sprinkling

¼ cup curly parsley

1½ cups crème fraîche

8–10 cubes of crusty bread, such as sourdough, optional

1 (12-inch) frozen pie crust, thawed, for quiche variation

Method

Preheat the oven to 350°F.

Heat the butter in a large ovenproof skillet over medium heat. Add the leek and cook until soft, about 10 minutes. Add the mushrooms and salt and pepper to taste. Cook until the mushrooms are soft, about 8 minutes.

In a separate bowl, whisk the eggs with the gruyère, parsley, crème fraîche, and a healthy pinch of salt and pepper. Pour this egg mixture over the mushrooms. Add the cubed bread (if using).

Sprinkle with more gruyère and place in the oven until the center is cooked through, about 20 minutes.

For the quiche variation, omit the cubed bread but prepare all the other ingredients in the same way. Pour the egg mixture into the pie crust and bake according to the package instructions. Generally a quiche this size should take 45 minutes to bake, but watch for it to be fully set and test it by inserting a knife into the center of the quiche. If it comes out clean, it's cooked through.

TIP *Good fish markets typically sell most seafood accompaniments as well, so keep an eye out for horseradish, seafood sauce, tabasco, mayonnaise, and lemons!*

For us, there is nothing quite as opulent as a well-put-together raw bar, and bringing the raw bar experience into our home sets the tone for a truly memorable evening.

While preparing an entirely seafood-based meal may seem like a daunting task, by sticking to a clear, elegant menu and following our tips and tricks, you'll find that preparing a seafood extravaganza isn't nearly as complicated as it seems.

The main attraction of our seafood extravaganza is, of course, the seafood towers. If you don't have a seafood tower in your kitchen, get creative with platters, bowls, or cake stands to make a temporary tower to display your tasty seafood selections.

Many people are intimidated by the idea of hosting a seafood dinner because they overthink the preparation process. In this chapter, you'll learn how to focus on the most important aspects of your seafood extravaganza without stressing over the tiny details. It comes down to picking the freshest seafood and some good basic accompaniments, using lots of ice, and having a few good bottles of white wine on hand.

3 PULLING OUT ALL THE STOPS

SEAFOOD

EXTRAVAGANZA

SETTING

Starting with a crisp white tablecloth as the foundation, we like to use charger plates instead of place mats to maintain a touch of formality while also grounding the overall place setting. Without overplaying the nautical theme, which can end up looking kitschy, we blend elements like the wicker charger plates, blue-and-white dinner plates, and clear glasses to help create the perfect seaside look without going "overboard."

Since the seafood tower will be the main attraction on your table, it's important to consider your table layout in advance and make sure all guests are within arm's reach of the tower. Keep in mind that, unlike the other dishes in this book that are meant to be shared, you can't pass a seafood tower around the table! For larger groups, 8 to 10 guests or more, we like to arrange the seafood on two separate towers.

For accent elements we use simple lanterns at both ends of the table to add light while playing into the oceanside theme. LED or wax candles both work well, but we prefer using LED candles as they don't blow out in the wind and make for an easy cleanup.

We accent each place setting with an individual set of accoutrements including a mini bottle of Tabasco and a freshly cut lemon wrapped in cheesecloth. It isn't always necessary to use cheesecloth, but we try to incorporate it whenever possible to prevent seeds from falling onto the food. For an added personal touch, try attaching a small place card to each setting. Finally, we set each place setting in a small rice bowl so guests have somewhere to keep their lemon in between uses or discard any shells.

TIP

A little trick we often use when entertaining outdoors is to set the table with all the plates and glasses turned over, so nothing falls into or onto them. There's no need to turn them the right way up until a couple of minutes before your guests arrive.

SHEILA SAYS *If you choose to add crab to your seafood tower, you can either go with crab claws or crab meat. Some people may be turned off by crab meat as it comes in a can, but as long as you buy high-quality jumbo lump crab meat, I'm sure you will be pleasantly surprised. Your local fishmonger (or the fish counter at your local grocery store) is a great resource. Ask them about the crab options and what they recommend. Of all the grocery store staff, it's always the butcher and the fishmonger who are best to "buddy up to"!*

WHAT'S ON THE MENU

We begin our seafood extravaganza with Chilled Cucumber Soup Shooters. This crisp and smooth amuse-bouche can be made a couple days before your dinner party and stored in your fridge. Serving it in small glasses instead of bowls will help save you cleanup time (glasses take up less space in the dishwasher than bowls!).

Another canapé that we love to incorporate into our seafood extravaganza dinners is Tuna Crostini. While these may not have the same flair as the rest of the dishes you have planned for the evening, they contribute to the coastal feel while serving as the perfect transition into your plated courses.

COURSES

Even though we are serving our guests some tasty canapés while they settle in, we still like to offer a traditional appetizer for when we transition to the table. Keeping with the seafood theme, we are serving a grilled calamari salad. Preparing this dish is a snap, since the salad can be tossed, plated, and then set aside while you quickly cook the calamari.

Once the appetizer is cleared, we get to our pièce de résistance and the main feature of the night: the seafood tower. The great thing about seafood towers is that they can be personalized according to your palate. For a meal for 6–8 people, we typically recommend choosing a maximum of 4–5 varieties of seafood and shellfish.

If this is your first time preparing a seafood tower, try sticking to shrimp, lobster, or crab, and one or two types of oysters. When it comes to quantities, we suggest buying 2–4 oysters, 3–4 tiger shrimp, and 1 lobster tail or 2 crab claws (or 3–4 oz of crab meat), depending on size, per person.

For some added variety, or if you plan on hosting a larger group, try adding lump crab meat, steamed and chilled mussels or clams, or even whelks (sea snails) to fill out the menu. When it comes to seafood towers, presentation is key. Think about how you'd like to organize your towers to give them balance in terms of flavor, texture, and aesthetics.

Seafood can be filling, especially when you offer so much variety, so we like to end the meal with a light dessert. For this menu we are serving a simple Raspberry Sorbet. Presented in a champagne coupe or martini glass and garnished with mint, this refreshing dessert is the perfect palate cleanser to close out your meal. It can be prepared a few days in advance and kept in the freezer until ready to serve.

SEB SAYS

If you're pressed for time, ask the fishmonger to boil or steam the lobsters, shrimp, and any other seafood that is served cooked. For certain items, like shrimp, you can also buy high-quality frozen poached versions. Just thaw before serving.

WHAT'S ON THE BAR

Our featured cocktail for this meal is a sparkling Kir Royale. Served in a champagne flute and garnished with raspberries, this cocktail features sparkling wine or prosecco with a small splash of crème de cassis or chambord. Anything bubbly is perfect to serve with seafood but a Kir Royale really sets the stage for an elegant and luxurious night.

As you and your guests transition to the table, we suggest serving cold, crisp white wines like a French chablis or Italian pinot grigio. When serving seafood, you want to stick with a light white wine, or rosé if it's summertime, to help brighten the flavor of the seafood. Avoid heavy white wines with more buttery notes (like chardonnays), as they tend to overpower the delicate seafood.

The key to serving a good white wine is getting the temperature right. Make sure the bottle remains tableside in a large ice bucket for the entirety of the meal. We always have extra ice on hand to replenish the bucket in case the ice starts to melt. An extra tip is to add some salt to your ice. This lowers the freezing point of the ice so, as it starts to melt, the water will actually be just as cold as the ice.

I love assembling seafood towers. My style is to keep oysters (usually two types) on the top tray with the mignonette sauces and perhaps some horseradish and cocktail sauce. I then fan out the lobster, crab, and shrimp on the lower tray with the appropriate garnishes. This makes it easier to remove the top tray once the oysters are done and refill it with freshly shucked oysters in the kitchen.

SEAFOOD EXTRAVAGANZA

COCKTAIL

KIR ROYALE (P288)

CANAPÉS

CHILLED CUCUMBER SOUP SHOOTERS (P289)

TUNA CROSTINI (P289)

APPETIZER

GRILLED CALAMARI SALAD (P290)

MAIN COURSE

SEAFOOD TOWER (P293)

CLASSIC MIGNONETTE SAUCE (P295)

WHITE MIGNONETTE SAUCE (P295)

SWEETS

RASPBERRY SORBET (P297)

PARTY COUNTDOWN:

SEAFOOD EXTRAVAGANZA

3 THREE DAYS BEFORE

○ Send a reminder email or text to your guests with details about the evening.

○ Make your grocery and alcohol lists.

○ Look through your inventory for suitable platters for the seafood tower.

○ Make sure you have enough seafood crackers and oyster forks.

○ Grocery shop (but leave the seafood and baguette for now) and stock up at the liquor store.

○ If champagne flutes and coupes don't get a lot of use in your house, check to see if they need a quick wash.

○ Make the salad dressing for the grilled calamari salad and refrigerate in an airtight container.

○ Make the raspberry sorbet and freeze.

2 TWO DAYS BEFORE

○ Make the mignonette sauces and refrigerate in an airtight container.

○ Make the chilled cucumber soup and refrigerate in an airtight container. If the soup separates, just give it a good stir before serving.

TIME-SAVING TIPS

Use store-bought mignonette sauces. You get what you pay for with these, though, so buy the best you can afford.

There are many high-quality sorbets available that taste just as fresh as our homemade version, so go store-bought if you prefer.

If you're pressed for time, canned lump crab is a great alternative to fresh.

Omit the calamari rings from the grilled calamari salad for a refreshing citrus salad to start the meal.

1 — THE DAY BEFORE

- ○ Make the tapenade for the tuna toasts.
- ○ Cut the cheesecloth for the lemons and write your place cards.

0 — THE DAY OF

- ○ Buy or pick up the fresh seafood.
- ○ Buy a fresh baguette for the tuna toasts.
- ○ Steam any seafood that needs to be cooked, then refrigerate under a clean, moist dish cloth.
- ○ Buy crushed ice, or buy regular ice and crush it yourself.
- ○ Assemble the seafood tower (check the timing on page 293).
- ○ Grill the calamari for the salad.
- ○ The lemons must be freshly cut, so assemble the cheesecloth-wrapped lemons just before your guests arrive.

KIR ROYALE

COCKTAIL +
CANAPÉS

TUNA CROSTINI

KIR ROYALE

yield: makes 1 cocktail · prep time: 5 minutes

Ingredients
6 oz prosecco or sparkling wine
½ oz crème de cassis
1 raspberry, for garnish

Method
Pour the prosecco into a champagne flute, top with the crème de cassis, and garnish with the raspberry.

SHEILA SAYS

Since Kir Royales are essentially sparkling wine and cassis liqueur, you can adjust the quantity of cassis to your preference. I like only a splash of cassis for color, but some people like a touch more because it adds a sweetness to the otherwise tart sparkling wine.

CHILLED CUCUMBER
SOUP SHOOTERS

yield: serves 6–8 · prep time: 20 minutes + 1½ hours
to chill

Ingredients

2 English cucumbers, peeled and seeded
¼ cup sour cream
2 Tbsp plain Greek yogurt
1 small garlic clove, minced
¼ cup olive oil + more for garnish
½ lemon, zest and juice of
Sea salt
Dill leaves, for garnish
Persian cucumber, sliced in ¼-inch rounds,
　for garnish

Method

Place the English cucumbers, sour cream, and yogurt
in a blender and pulse until blended. Add the garlic,
oil, and lemon zest and juice, and purée until smooth.
Season to taste with salt. Refrigerate for at least
1½ hours to chill, or in an airtight container for up
to 3 days.

When you're ready to serve, pour the soup into the
chilled shot glasses and garnish with dill leaves and
a few drops of oil. Slice each Persian cucumber
round halfway through and let it hang off the rim
of the glass.

TUNA CROSTINI

yield: serves 6–8 · prep time: 30 minutes ·
cook time: 10 minutes

Ingredients
CROSTINI
1 baguette
Olive oil, for brushing

TUNA
1 (5 oz) can tuna packed in olive oil
1 anchovy fillet packed in oil
1 small garlic clove, coarsely chopped
2 Tbsp flat-leaf parsley, divided
1 tsp thyme leaves
1½ tsp grated lemon zest
2 Tbsp mascarpone
2 Tbsp olive oil
1 Tbsp lemon juice
1 Tbsp mayonnaise
½ tsp black pepper
½ cup whole pitted black olives
1 Tbsp capers, divided
6 pitted black olives, quartered, for garnish

Method
FOR THE CROSTINI
Preheat the oven to 375°F.

Cut the baguette into ½-inch-thick slices on a slight
bias. Brush each side with oil and bake until golden
brown, about 10 minutes, flipping halfway through.
Remove from the oven and let cool completely.

FOR THE TUNA
Drain the tuna to remove most of the oil. Place it in
a food processor fitted with the steel blade and add
the anchovy, garlic, 1½ Tbsp of the parsley, the
thyme, and lemon zest. Pulse to combine. Add the
mascarpone, oil, lemon juice, mayonnaise, and pepper. Process on high speed until it forms a thick,
homogeneous paste. Add the whole pitted black
olives and 1½ tsp of the capers and pulse until just
combined, leaving a few pieces visible. Refrigerate in
an airtight container up to overnight.

TO SERVE
Spread about 1 Tbsp of the tuna mixture on each
toast and garnish with a few olive quarters, a few
capers, and a sprinkling of the remaining parsley.

GRILLED CALAMARI SALAD

yield: serves 6 · prep time: 30 minutes · cook time: 5 minutes

Ingredients

CALAMARI

2 lb cleaned calamari
(1 tube + 1 tentacle per guest)

3 Tbsp olive oil

Sea salt and black pepper

DRESSING

¾ cup avocado oil

3 Tbsp lemon juice

2 Tbsp rice wine vinegar

Sea salt and black pepper

SALAD

6 cups blended mixed greens
(sprouts optional)

6 lime wedges

6 slices preserved hot peppers,
packed in oil

Sea salt and black pepper

Method

FOR THE CALAMARI
Preheat the grill to high. Pat the calamari dry with paper towels and score each side of the tubes, being careful not to cut them all the way through.

In a small bowl, toss the calamari with the oil and salt and pepper to taste.

Grill the calamari until firm and opaque, about 1 minute per side. Remove from the grill, allow to cool, then slice into ¼-inch-thick rings.

FOR THE DRESSING
Whisk together the oil, lemon juice, vinegar, and salt and pepper to taste in a small bowl until completely combined.

FOR THE SALAD
Place the greens on a plate. Arrange the calamari rings, lime wedges, and chilies on the side so that the heat of the calamari doesn't wilt the salad greens. Season lightly with salt and pepper and drizzle with dressing.

Note
If you're making this ahead of time, the grilled calamari can be refrigerated in an airtight container and sliced into rings just before serving. The dressing can be refrigerated in a glass jar for up to 5 days.

SEAFOOD TOWER

yield: serves 6–8 · prep time: 30 minutes + overnight to thaw + overnight to chill · cook time: 45 minutes

Ingredients

COURT BOUILLON

1 yellow onion, peeled, quartered

2 stalks celery, quartered

1 large carrot, cut in 3-inch pieces

¾ cup coarsely chopped fennel
    bulb

1 lemon, quartered

4 bay leaves

2 Tbsp sea salt

1 Tbsp whole black peppercorns

SEAFOOD TOWER

10 bamboo skewers

10 (each 6 oz) lobster tails, thawed
    overnight if frozen (see note)

24 frozen crab claws, thawed
    overnight (see note)

24 jumbo shrimp (13/15 count),
    shells on

1 lb lump crab meat

6 lemons, each cut into 8 wedges

2 cups seafood sauce

1 cup grated horseradish

1 cup mayonnaise

Classic Mignonette Sauce
    (page 295)

White Mignonette Sauce (page 295)

24 medium oysters, shucked

Note

It's always best to slowly thaw the frozen seafood components rather than trying to rush the thawing with cold water (which absorbs into the meat). We like to place the frozen items in the fridge overnight on a tray lined with paper towel so it absorbs any of the moisture from the items, then leave for 15 minutes at room temperature on fresh paper towel to dry before assembling the tower.

Method

FOR THE COURT BOUILLON

Fill a large stockpot with 5 quarts of water and add the onions, celery, carrots, fennel, lemon, bay leaves, salt, and peppercorns. Bring to a boil over high heat, then reduce the heat to medium and simmer, uncovered, for 20 minutes.

Strain and discard the solids from the court bouillon and return the stock to a boil.

FOR THE SEAFOOD TOWER

Insert a bamboo skewer through the length of each lobster tail. Poach each lobster tail in the court bouillon for 9 minutes. Remove from the poaching liquid, allow the lobster tails to come to room temperature, then refrigerate for at least 8 hours, or overnight.

To serve, remove and discard the skewer and split the lobster meat lengthwise in its shell. To do this, turn the tail on its back and insert the tip of large knife into the top portion of the meat, slowly lowering the knife to pierce the soft underside of the tail from top to bottom, exposing the meat.

To prepare the crab claws, set a steamer basket in a large pot and fill it with water, ensuring that the water doesn't touch the bottom of the basket. Add the crab claws, cover with a lid, and steam until claws are bright red, about 5 minutes.

To prepare the shrimp, fill a pot with water and bring it to a boil over high heat. Add the shrimp and cook uncovered for 1–2 minutes. Cover, remove from the heat, and let the shrimp sit in the pot of hot water to continue cooking until pink and opaque, about 5 minutes. If you buy frozen pre-cooked shrimp you can skip this step and just thaw them (the same goes for the lobster and crab claws).

TO ASSEMBLE

Before you put anything on your tower, place it in the freezer for at least 1 hour. Line your tower tiers with an even layer of crushed ice.

Arrange the cooked shrimp, crab claws, crab meat, and lobster over the ice on the lower tier, leaving the top tray for the oysters. This placement makes it easy to remove the top tray once the oysters are done and refill it with freshly shucked ones from the kitchen.

Once you've placed your larger pieces of seafood on the tower, fill in the gaps with the smaller pieces and lemon wedges. If you have space, place the seafood sauce, horseradish, mayonnaise, and mignonette sauces in several small bowls directly on the ice and surround them with seafood. If not, simply serve them on the table beside the towers.

Shuck the oysters immediately before serving and place them on the top trays of the towers.

CLASSIC MIGNONETTE SAUCE

yield: ½ cup · prep time: 10 minutes + 1 hour to marinate

Ingredients

½ cup red wine vinegar
1 shallot, finely chopped
½ tsp black pepper

Method

In a small bowl, whisk together the vinegar, shallot, and pepper until completely combined. Allow to sit for at least 1 hour at room temperature to let the flavors develop. Otherwise, refrigerate in an airtight container for up to 2 days.

WHITE MIGNONETTE SAUCE

yield: 1¼ cup · prep time: 20 minutes + 1 hour to marinate

Ingredients

½ cup champagne vinegar
¼ shallot, finely chopped
¼ cup finely diced peeled green apple
¼ cup finely diced fennel bulb
1 tsp granulated sugar
White pepper

Method

In a small bowl, whisk together the vinegar, shallot, apple, fennel, sugar, and a pinch of pepper until completely combined. Allow to sit for at least 1 hour at room temperature to let the flavors develop. Otherwise, refrigerate in an airtight container for up to 2 days.

RASPBERRY SORBET

yield: makes 2 cups · prep time: 20 minutes + 2 hours to chill · cook time: 5 minutes

Ingredients

MINT SIMPLE SYRUP
½ cup granulated sugar
8 mint leaves

SORBET
3 cups frozen raspberries
1 Tbsp honey
½ lemon, zest and juice of
⅓ cup mint simple syrup
Mint leaves, for garnish
Fresh raspberries, for garnish

Method

FOR THE SIMPLE SYRUP

In a small saucepan over medium-high heat, bring ½ cup of water, the sugar, and mint leaves to a boil. Reduce the heat to low and simmer, uncovered, stirring occasionally, until the sugar is fully dissolved, 5 minutes. Remove from the heat and allow to cool completely. Strain the syrup into an airtight container and discard the mint leaves. Refrigerate for up to 1 week.

FOR THE SORBET

Place the raspberries, honey, and lemon zest and juice in a food processor fitted with the steel blade. Pulse just until the raspberries are broken into small pieces.

With the food processor running, pour in the simple syrup in a slow, continuous stream until the mixture is fully blended. Add warm water, 1 Tbsp at a time, if necessary to achieve a creamy texture.

Freeze in a freezer-safe airtight container for at least 2 hours, or overnight. Serve in a champagne coupe or martini glass. Garnish with the mint and fresh raspberries.

ACKNOWLEDGMENTS

There are so many people we need to acknowledge and thank since this book would never have come to be without them.

To our kids first: Colsen Centner, who worked tirelessly to help write the drafts of our chapters (no small feat when working from our notes), and Logan Centner, who, while not directly involved in the production of the book, was always there to help Sheila recipe test our cocktails and play photographer for our countless BTS shoots for social media. As young children, Colsen and Logan suffered through many nights of trying to fall asleep (or stay asleep) while their parents hosted dinners that most often turned into impromptu dance parties lasting until the wee hours. Luckily, they grew up appreciating our passion for hosting and have each caught the entertaining bug, taking part in our entertaining life and even hosting their own friends. We love you both so much and can't wait to come to dinner parties at your houses for a change!

To our friends who joined us for the many photoshoots: the shoots were certainly fun and delicious but nobody will ever appreciate the patience you displayed through all the shooting and re-shooting. We made it through, with the light at the end of the tunnel being a great meal and lots of delicious cocktails to enjoy!

To Bruce Gibson, the most talented, professional, and easy-to-work with photographer in the business: we've talked about this project for over a decade with you and now you've brought it to life for us! We've done over 100 shoots with Bruce over the years and we're looking forward to the next 100. Bruce is not only a master of his craft but also the kindest, most accommodating photographer and a dear friend. To Bruce's assistants, Eric Yeh and Blake Cathcart, thank you for your tireless efforts on the long shoots, in the blistering heat and the piercing cold! www.brucegibsonphotography.com @brucemgibson

To Chris Matthews, the executive chef at Eatertainment. com and a loyal team member of ours for over a decade: we cannot thank you enough for your creativity in bringing our menus to life and providing expert advice on how to best share easy-to-follow recipes for this book.

To Victoria Gibson, who played an indispensable behind-the-scenes role at every photoshoot and is the driving force behind the social media for us and our businesses. Victoria's creativity and passion for all things entertaining quickly made her a key part of our team, and her support for our wild schedules and often last-minute decisions on social media strategies will never be forgotten. When it comes to rising to the occasion, we've never seen better!

To Enza Cammalleri, who came out of our past as the producer of the photoshoots and recipes in this book: your commitment to finding just the right props and ingredients for our shoots, testing (and re-testing) our recipes, and working with our editor to ensure every recipe was accurate and easy to follow is matched only by the creativity you brought to this book with your passion for cooking.

To Kris Rushton, Chris Wies, and Kenneth Holt: three of the most talented chefs we have ever had the pleasure to work with and who each played important roles in bringing the food dishes to life in the dozens of photoshoots that it took to make this book.

To the entire Eatertainment team who helped pull off these shoots but more importantly, who make each of our events a world-class one and tend to the hundreds of details that go into running a catering and event company that hosts over 1700 events a year: Jackie Brown, Kori Gorman, Louise Reilly, Julianna Csiszar, Suzanne Dunbar, and the dozens of event managers, chefs, delivery staff and support teams—you guys are the best! www.eatertainment.com @eatertainment

A very special thanks to Tim and Laurie Foote (and their amazing daughter Tessa), who hosted us so many times at their stunning Windswept Farm in Creemore and gave us the privilege of shooting the chapters Fall Harvest Linner and Winter Warm-Up at their beautiful property. Laurie and Tessa were always there to help us pull off the shoot, being culinary creatives themselves with their Two Dirty Aprons blogs and pop-up markets! www.2dirtyaprons.com @2dirtyaprons

To Sally and Detlef Doerge, some of our dearest friends and the most consummate hosts we will ever meet. Not only have you hosted us more times than we can count, but you were so kind to provide the stunning setting of your home in which to shoot our chapters A Mussels Dinner and A Mediterranean Lunch. Your home and family epitomize the spirit of entertaining and we are lucky to count you among our closest friends. You have opened your home, your family, and your wine cellar to us, and for that we will always be thankful. Full disclosure: it is Sally (one of the most unbelievable cooks we know) and Detlef (one of the heaviest-pouring bartenders we know) from whom we borrowed the phrase "our door only opens inward!"

To Sylvia Baumann and Glenn Shyba, whom we have known for a lifetime and who have shared with us many a night filled with great food, laughter, and, of course, the somewhat inappropriate game of charades at their stunning cottage and our respective homes. You were there for the first Eve Before The Eve, and will be there for every one to come. Thank you for also allowing us the use of your home to shoot the chapters Cocktail Party 101, Fun with Kids, and Easy Al Fresco Dinner.

Thank you to our amazing partners and suppliers!

Anne Grealis at Event Rental Group and Marni Berman and Lee-Ann Tait at Chairman Mills. As partners of ours and Eatertainment's for over two decades, you not only brought our shoots to life with all the amazing tableware and props from the two best event rental companies in the country, but also have shown unwavering support for our business. Whether it's an event for 4000 people or finding a way to get us that extra teapot at the last minute on a Saturday morning, we know Anne and her team will answer the call as the consummate professionals they are. www.eventrentalgroup.com @eventrentalgroup and www.chairmanmills.com @chairmanmills

Miki at Blooms Plus: the most talented florist in the country and one of the kindest people we've ever worked with, thank you for the stunning florals that adorn the pages of this book. www.bloomsplus.ca @bloomsplus

To our fantastic team at Appetite by Random House. Zoe Maslow, thank you for the hours and hours (and hours) you spent working with us to turn basic words and images into this amazing book—your patience as you taught us the ins and outs of publishing is well deserving of several bottles of rosé together soon! Robert McCullough, thank you for believing in our vision and giving us the opportunity to make this dream come true. Thank you also for putting up with our preambles and pre-preambles when we were passionate about an issue, and for always providing amazing guidance and direction in the most professional way! Jennifer Griffiths, thank you for your creativity in laying out and designing this book: it's made all the difference to the end product. To Josh Glover, who brought this project to Appetite in the first place, believing that our entertaining passion should be shared: We cannot thank you enough. From that first conversation many years ago, to always being there to bounce ideas off, you have been a champion of ours through this entire process. And thank you to Lesley Cameron, our copyeditor, whose contributions to making sure all the little inconsistencies got caught before our final manuscript went to print is hugely appreciated. www.penguinrandomhouse.ca @appetite_randomhouse

INDEX